MW00888020

Understanding Catholicism

Exploring the Sacred Traditions of
Catholic Belief and Practice

DAVID M. EATON

Contents

CHAPTER 1

Introduction to Catholicism

Like most people, you have likely heard about the Catholic religion, but how much do you really know about it?

Put simply, Catholicism is one of the largest and most influential branches of Christianity, with a rich history and a significant global presence. It is a faith tradition that traces its roots back to the teachings of Jesus Christ and the establishment of the early Christian Church. In this book, we will explore the key aspects of Catholicism, including its beliefs, practices, organization, and impact on society.

At the core of Catholicism is the belief in the Holy Trinity, which encompasses the belief in one God who exists in three persons: the Father, the Son (Jesus Christ), and the Holy Spirit. Catholics believe that Jesus Christ is the Son of God, who became incarnate, lived a sinless life, died on the cross for the redemption of humanity, and rose from the dead. They also believe in the authority of the Bible, as well as the teachings of the Church, which are guided by the Holy Spirit.

Catholic worship is centered around the celebration of the sacraments, which are considered sacred rituals that convey God's grace to the faithful. The seven sacraments include Baptism, Confirmation, Eucharist (also known as the Holy Communion), Reconciliation (Confession), Anointing of the Sick, Holy Orders (ordination of priests and bishops), and Matrimony (marriage). The Eucharist, in particular, holds a central place in Catholic worship, as it is believed to be the actual body and blood of Christ.

The Catholic Church is led by the Pope, who is considered the successor of Saint Peter, the first Pope. The Pope is regarded as the spiritual leader and the head of the worldwide Catholic Church. Underneath the Pope, there is a hierarchical structure that includes cardinals, bishops, priests, and deacons. The Church is organized into dioceses, each headed by a bishop, and parishes, which are local communities of worship.

Throughout history, Catholicism has been known for its rich traditions and devotions that have developed over centuries. These include the veneration of saints, the use of sacramentals (such as holy water and rosary beads), and the practice of praying the Rosary. The liturgical calendar, which follows the life of Christ and the saints, is also an important aspect of Catholic tradition, with various feasts and celebrations throughout the year.

The religion places a strong emphasis on social justice and moral teachings. The Church teaches that all human life is sacred and should be protected from conception to natural death. It advocates for the dignity and rights of every individual, including the poor, marginalized, and vulnerable. Catholic social teaching addresses issues such as poverty, immigration, human rights, and the environment.

Throughout history, Catholicism has played a significant role in shaping Western civilization and has had a profound impact on art, literature, education, and politics alike. The Catholic Church has been a major patron of the arts, with magnificent cathedrals, sculptures, paintings, and music that reflect its spiritual and cultural heritage. Catholic educational institutions, such as universities and schools, have contributed to the advancement of knowledge and learning. The Church has also been involved in various social and humanitarian initiatives, including healthcare, charitable works, and advocacy for peace and justice.

Basic Beliefs and Practices

Throughout this book, we will explore the beliefs and practices of Catholicism, but let's briefly sum them up here:

- **Belief in the Holy Trinity:** Central to Catholicism is the belief in the Holy Trinity, which holds that God exists as three distinct persons—the Father, the Son (Jesus Christ), and the Holy Spirit—while remaining one God. This belief reflects the mystery of God's nature and underscores the unity and diversity within the divine.

- **Authority of Scripture and Tradition:** Catholics believe in the authority of both Sacred Scripture and Sacred Tradition. The Bible is considered the inspired Word of God, containing the teachings and stories that guide the faith. Additionally, Sacred Tradition, which includes the teachings passed down by the apostles and the early Church, is seen as a complementary source of divine revelation.

- **Salvation through Jesus Christ:** Belief in the redemptive work of Jesus Christ, who, through his life, death, and resurrection, offers salvation to humanity. It is through faith in Christ and participation in the sacraments that Catholics believe they can receive God's grace and attain eternal life.

- **The Seven Sacraments:** Sacraments are sacred rituals instituted by Christ that convey God's grace to the faithful. Catholicism recognizes seven sacraments: Baptism, Confirmation, Eucharist, Reconciliation (Confession), Anointing of the Sick, Holy Orders, and Matrimony. These sacraments are seen as tangible signs of God's presence and transformative power in the lives of believers.

- **The Eucharist:** The Eucharist, also known as the Holy Communion or the Lord's Supper, holds a central place in Catholic worship. Catholics believe that during the Mass, the bread and wine used in the sacrament of the Eucharist become the actual body and blood of Christ, while retaining the appearance of bread and wine. This belief in the Real Presence of Christ is a distinctive aspect of Catholic theology.

- **Devotion to Mary and the Saints:** Catholics hold a special reverence for Mary, the mother of Jesus, whom they honor as the Mother of God. Mary is seen as a model of faith and intercessor for believers. Additionally, Catholics venerate the saints, who are considered holy men and women who have lived exemplary lives of faith and are believed to be in the presence of God. Saints serve as intercessors and sources of inspiration for Catholics.

- **Moral Teachings and Social Justice:** Catholicism places a strong emphasis on moral teachings and social justice. Catholics are called to live according to the moral principles outlined in the Ten Commandments and the teachings of Jesus. The Church's social teachings address issues such as human dignity, social justice, care for the poor and vulnerable, and the promotion of peace and reconciliation.

- **Worship and Liturgy:** Catholic worship is characterized by liturgical celebrations, which include the Mass, the Liturgy of the Hours, and various devotional practices. The Mass, considered the highest form of worship, follows a structured order, and includes readings from Scripture, prayers, hymns, and the reception of the Eucharist. The liturgical calendar, with its feasts and seasons, guides the rhythm of Catholic worship throughout the year.

- **Prayer and Personal Devotion:** Followers engage in various forms of prayer and personal devotion to deepen their relationship with God. These practices include vocal prayers, such as the Our Father and the Hail Mary, as well as contemplative prayer, meditation, and the use of devotional aids like the Rosary and Stations of the Cross.

- **Reconciliation and Spiritual Direction:** Catholics have the opportunity to seek forgiveness and reconciliation through the sacrament of Reconciliation (Confession). This sacrament allows individuals to confess their sins to a priest, receive absolution, and experience spiritual healing. Additionally, spiritual direction, the guidance of a spiritual director, is available to help individuals deepen their spiritual journey and discern God's will.

These beliefs and practices shape the spiritual life of Catholics and provide a framework for living out their faith in the world.

CHAPTER 2

History of Catholicism

T he early development and spread of Catholicism can be traced back to the time of Jesus Christ and the establishment of the early Christian Church. This period marked the foundation of the faith and the subsequent growth and expansion of the Catholic Church throughout the Roman Empire and beyond.

Following the crucifixion and resurrection of Jesus Christ, his disciples, led by Saint Peter and the other apostles, formed the core of the early Christian community. They spread the teachings of Jesus and established Christian communities in various regions, primarily in the eastern Mediterranean.

In the early centuries, Christianity faced persecution from the Roman Empire, which viewed it as a threat to its authority. Christians were often subjected to harsh treatment, including imprisonment, torture, and execution. Despite this persecution, the faith continued to grow, and the courage and steadfastness of the martyrs became a powerful witness to the Christian message.

In the early 4th century, Emperor Constantine's conversion to Christianity marked a significant turning point for the faith. In 313 AD, Constantine issued the Edict of Milan, granting religious tolerance to Christians and ending the persecution. This newfound acceptance allowed Christianity to flourish and gain prominence within the Roman Empire.

As the Christian community expanded, the need for doctrinal clarity and unity arose. Ecumenical councils, such as the Council of Nicaea in 325 AD, were convened to address theological disputes and establish orthodox beliefs. These councils played a crucial role in shaping the early foundations of Catholic doctrine, including the affirmation of the divinity of Christ and the formulation of the Nicene Creed.

The Bishop of Rome, who later became known as the Pope, emerged as a central figure in the leadership of the Church. The Pope's authority and role as the successor of Saint Peter were gradually recognized, solidifying the hierarchical structure of the Catholic Church. The papacy provided stability and leadership during a time of political and social upheaval.

The rise of monasticism in the 4th century brought about a new wave of spiritual fervor and missionary activity. Monastic communities, such as those established by Saint Benedict, played a vital role in preserving knowledge, promoting education, and spreading the Christian faith. Monks and missionaries ventured into new territories, bringing Christianity to regions beyond the Roman Empire, such as Ireland, England, and the Germanic tribes.

The fall of the Western Roman Empire in the 5th century led to the migration and settlement of various barbarian tribes in Europe. The Catholic Church played a significant role in the conversion of these tribes to Christianity. Missionaries, such as Saint Patrick in Ireland and Saint Boniface in Germany, worked tirelessly to spread the faith and establish Christian communities among these newly converted peoples.

During the reign of Charlemagne in the 8th and 9th centuries, the Catholic Church experienced a period of revival and cultural renaissance known as the Carolingian Renaissance. Charlemagne's support for education, the arts, and the Church's mission led to the preservation and dissemination of knowledge, the standardization of liturgical practices, and the spread of Christianity throughout his empire.

In the 11th to 13th centuries, the Catholic Church was instrumental in the Crusades, a series of military campaigns aimed at reclaiming the Holy Land from Muslim control. While the Crusades had complex motivations and consequences, they contributed to the expansion of Catholic influence and the spread of Western Christianity.

During the Age of Exploration in the 15th and 16th centuries, Catholic missionaries accompanied European explorers to newly discovered lands. They sought to convert indigenous peoples to Christianity, resulting in the spread of Catholicism to regions such as the Americas, Africa, and Asia. This period marked a significant global expansion of the Catholic Church.

This was quickly followed by the Protestant Reformation, initiated by Martin Luther in the 16th century, challenging certain practices and doctrines of the Catholic Church. This movement led to the splintering of Christianity into various Protestant denominations and brought about significant changes within Catholicism through the Counter-Reformation. Hence, key figures of the Reformation, such as Martin Luther, John Calvin, and Huldrych Zwingli, played a pivotal role in shaping the religious landscape of Europe.

The Council of Trent, held between 1545 and 1563, was a response to the challenges posed by the Protestant Reformation. This ecumenical council addressed doctrinal issues, reaffirmed Catholic teachings, and initiated reforms within the Church. The Council of Trent played a crucial role in solidifying Catholic doctrine and practices, shaping the faith for centuries to come.

We can then move to discuss The Second Vatican Council, convened between 1962 and 1965, a landmark event in modern Catholic history. This ecumenical council aimed to renew and update the Church's teachings and practices, promoting dialogue with other Christian denominations and addressing contemporary issues. The council resulted in significant changes, including liturgical reforms, increased emphasis on ecumenism, and a renewed focus on the role of the laity.

Of course, throughout Catholic history, numerous saints and religious orders have made significant contributions to the faith. Figures such as Saint Augustine, Saint Thomas Aquinas, Saint Teresa of Avila, and Saint Francis of Assisi have left a lasting impact through their writings, teachings, and examples of holiness. Religious orders, such as the Benedictines, Franciscans, Dominicans, and Jesuits, have played a vital role in the spiritual and intellectual life of the Church.

Major Schisms and Reforms Within Catholicism

Throughout its history, Catholicism has experienced significant schisms and undergone transformative reforms that have shaped the development and evolution of the faith. These events have had profound consequences for the Catholic Church, leading to theological, cultural, and institutional changes. While we have learned about the timeline of Catholicism, let's now turn our attention to the major schisms and reforms that have occurred through the years.

Pulling these apart provides us with insights into the challenges and transformations that have shaped Catholicism over the centuries.

- **The Great Schism of 1054:** The Great Schism marked a significant division within Christianity, resulting in the separation of the Roman Catholic Church in the West and the Eastern Orthodox Church in the East. The schism was primarily driven by theological, cultural, and political differences between the Latin-speaking West and the Greek-speaking East. The mutual excommunications between the Pope and the Patriarch of Constantinople symbolized the formal split between the two branches of Christianity. This schism had lasting consequences, leading to the development of distinct theological traditions and ecclesiastical structures in the East and the West.

- **The Protestant Reformation:** The Protestant Reformation, initiated by Martin Luther in the 16th century, challenged certain practices and doctrines of the Catholic Church. Luther's Ninety-Five Theses, which criticized the sale of indulgences and questioned the authority of the Pope, sparked a movement that led to the splintering of Christianity into various Protestant denominations. The Reformation brought about significant changes within Catholicism through the Counter-Reformation, a period of reform and renewal that addressed some of the concerns raised by the Protestant Reformers. The Council of Trent, held between 1545 and 1563, played a crucial role in reaffirming Catholic teachings, initiating reforms, and solidifying Catholic doctrine.

- **The Jansenist Controversy:** The Jansenist controversy emerged in the 17th century as a theological and ecclesiastical dispute within the Catholic Church. Jansenism, influenced by the teachings of Cornelius Jansen, emphasized the doctrine of predestination, and advocated for a rigorous moral and ascetic lifestyle. The movement faced opposition from the Church hierarchy, and its teachings were eventually condemned as heretical. The Jansenist controversy highlighted tensions between theological perspectives and the authority of the Church, contributing to debates on grace, free will, and the role of the individual in salvation.

- **The Modernist Crisis:** The Modernist crisis, which occurred in the late 19th and early 20th centuries, was a theological and intellectual movement that sought to reconcile Catholicism with modern thought and culture. Modernist theologians, influenced by philosophical and scientific developments, sought to reinterpret traditional Catholic teachings in light of contemporary knowledge. However, their ideas were met with resistance from the Church hierarchy, leading to condemnations and the suppression of Modernist writings. The crisis highlighted tensions between tradition and progress, faith and reason, and the role of intellectual inquiry within the Catholic Church.

- **Vatican II and Post-Vatican II Reforms:** The Second Vatican Council, held between 1962 and 1965, was a landmark event in modern Catholic history. The council aimed to renew and update the Church's teachings and practices, promoting dialogue with other Christian denominations and addressing contemporary issues. Vatican II resulted in significant changes, including liturgical reforms, increased emphasis on ecumenism, a renewed focus on the role of the laity, and a call for greater engagement with the modern world. Post-Vatican II reforms have continued to shape Catholicism, with ongoing discussions on topics such as social justice, interfaith dialogue, the role of women, and the interpretation of Catholic teachings.

These major schisms and reforms within Catholicism have challenged the Church, prompting theological reflection, institutional changes, and cultural adaptations. While they have caused divisions and tensions, they have also led to renewed spiritual vitality, a deeper understanding of the faith, and a more engaged relationship with the world. Catholicism continues to evolve and respond to the challenges of each era, guided by its rich tradition, the teachings of Jesus Christ, and the ongoing discernment of the Holy Spirit.

CHAPTER 3

The Catholic Church Structure

T he hierarchical structure of the Catholic Church is a complex system that provides organization, leadership, and governance to the worldwide community of Catholic believers. This structure is designed to ensure unity, promote the teachings of the Church, and facilitate the spiritual well-being of its members.

- **The Pope:** At the apex of the hierarchy is the Pope, who is considered the spiritual leader and the Vicar of Christ on Earth. Also known as the Bishop of Rome, the Pope is the head of the Catholic Church. He is believed to be the successor of Saint Peter, who was appointed by Jesus Christ as the leader of the apostles. The Pope holds supreme authority in matters of faith, morals, and Church governance. He is responsible for guiding the Church, making doctrinal decisions, and providing spiritual leadership to Catholics worldwide.

- **The College of Cardinals:** This is a body of senior clergy appointed by the Pope. Its primary function is to advise the Pope and elect a new Pope when the position becomes vacant. Cardinals are typically bishops or archbishops, and they hold various administrative and pastoral responsibilities within the Church. The College of Cardinals reflects the diversity of the global Catholic Church and plays a crucial role in the selection of the Pope.

- **The Roman Curia:** It is the administrative apparatus of the Catholic Church, assisting the Pope in the governance of the Church. It consists of various departments, known as dicasteries, which oversee different aspects of Church life. These dicasteries include the Secretariat of State, the Congregation for the Doctrine of the Faith, the Congregation for the Evangelization of Peoples, and the Congregation for the Clergy, among others. The Roman Curia ensures the smooth functioning of the Church's administrative and pastoral activities.

- **Bishops:** Holding the highest-ranking clergy within the Catholic Church, serving as the spiritual leaders of specific geographical regions known as dioceses, are bishops. Bishops are ordained through the sacrament of Holy Orders and are considered successors of the apostles.

- **Archbishops:** They are bishops who have been given additional responsibilities and authority within their respective regions. They oversee larger dioceses or archdioceses, which may have multiple smaller dioceses under their jurisdiction.

- **Priests:** Also known as presbyters, priests are ordained ministers who serve the spiritual needs of local communities within a diocese or parish. Priests are ordained through the sacrament of Holy Orders and are under the authority of their respective bishops.

- **Deacons:** They are ordained ministers who assist priests and bishops in their pastoral duties. Deacons can be either transitional, on the path to priesthood, or permanent, serving in a lifelong diaconal ministry.

- **Religious Orders:** Also known as religious congregations or religious communities, religious orders are groups of men or women who live a communal life dedicated to prayer, service, and the pursuit of holiness. These orders, such as the Franciscans, Dominicans, Jesuits, and Benedictines, have their own hierarchical structures and are governed by their respective superiors.

The hierarchical structure of the Catholic Church provides a framework for the organization, leadership, and governance of the faith community. It ensures the unity and continuity of the Church's teachings, facilitates the administration of sacraments, and promotes the spiritual well-being of Catholics worldwide. This structure reflects the belief in apostolic succession, the authority of the Pope, and the collaboration between clergy and laity in the mission of the Church.

Roles and Responsibilities of Clergy Members

Clergy members play a vital role in the Catholic Church, serving as spiritual leaders and ministers to the faithful. They are ordained individuals who have received the sacrament of Holy Orders and are entrusted with specific roles and responsibilities within the Church. These roles vary depending on the level of ordination, from deacons to priests and bishops. Understanding the distinct responsibilities of each clergy member provides insight into their contributions to the spiritual life of the Church.

- **Deacons:** Deacons serve the community, both within and outside the Church. They may be involved in various ministries, including preaching, administering sacraments such as baptism and marriage, and providing pastoral care to the sick and marginalized. They often have a particular focus on social justice and outreach, working to address the needs of the community and promote charitable initiatives.

- **Priests:** Their primary responsibilities include celebrating the sacraments, particularly the Eucharist, hearing confessions, and providing pastoral care to the faithful. Priests are called to preach the Gospel, teach the doctrines of the Church, and guide individuals in their spiritual journey. They often play a central role in the liturgical life of the Church, leading worship services, conducting weddings and funerals, and offering spiritual guidance and counseling to parishioners.

- **Bishops:** They provide pastoral care and governance to their dioceses. Bishops oversee the administration of sacraments, ensure the teaching of sound doctrine, and promote the spiritual well-being of the faithful. They are responsible for ordaining priests and deacons, confirming individuals, and maintaining unity within their dioceses. Bishops also play a role in the broader Church, participating in the governance of the Church through their involvement in synods and councils.

- **Archbishops:** Archbishops often play a significant role in the administration of the Church, including the ordination of priests, the coordination of pastoral activities, and the representation of their archdioceses in regional and national contexts. They work closely with bishops and priests to ensure the spiritual well-being of the faithful within their jurisdiction.

- **Religious Orders:** Members of religious orders, such as monks, nuns, and friars, have distinct roles and responsibilities within their communities. They live a communal life dedicated to prayer, service, and the pursuit of holiness. The specific responsibilities of members of religious orders vary depending on the charism and mission of their particular order. Some may focus on education, healthcare, social justice, or contemplative prayer. They contribute to the spiritual life of the Church through their commitment to their order's specific mission and their dedication to a life of prayer and service.

These clergy members, through their distinct roles and responsibilities, contribute to the spiritual well-being of the Catholic Church and its faithful. Whether serving as deacons, priests, bishops, or members of religious orders, they provide pastoral care, administer sacraments, preach the Gospel, and guide individuals in their spiritual journey. Their commitment to the teachings of the Church and their service to the community are essential in fostering the spiritual growth and well-being of the faithful.

Importance of the Vatican and the Pope

The Vatican and the Pope hold immense significance within the Catholic Church and have a profound impact on the spiritual lives of Catholics worldwide. They serve as symbols of unity, authority, and spiritual guidance, playing crucial roles in the governance, teachings, and representation of the Church. Thus, understanding the importance of the Vatican and the Pope provides insight into the central structures and leadership of the Catholic faith.

- **Spiritual Leadership:** The Pope, as the Bishop of Rome and the head of the Catholic Church, is considered the spiritual leader and the Vicar of Christ on Earth. He is believed to be the successor of Saint Peter, who was appointed by Jesus Christ as the leader of the apostles. The Pope's spiritual leadership is seen as a continuation of the apostolic tradition, providing guidance, inspiration, and moral authority to Catholics worldwide. The Pope's teachings and pronouncements on matters of faith, morals, and social issues carry significant weight and influence within the Church.

- **Unity and Authority:** The Vatican, located within the city-state of Vatican City, serves as the central governing body of the Catholic Church. It is the residence of the Pope and the administrative headquarters of the Church. The Vatican plays a crucial role in maintaining unity and coherence within the Church, ensuring that the teachings and practices of Catholicism are upheld worldwide. The Pope, as the highest authority within the Church, exercises his leadership from the Vatican, making decisions, issuing encyclicals, and providing pastoral guidance to the faithful. The Vatican's authority extends to matters of doctrine, liturgy, canon law, and the appointment of bishops and cardinals.

- **Preservation of Tradition and Doctrine:** The Vatican, through its various departments and congregations, is responsible for preserving and promoting the traditions, doctrines, and teachings of the Catholic Church. It ensures the integrity and fidelity of Catholic teachings, safeguarding the deposit of faith passed down through the centuries. The Vatican's role in maintaining orthodoxy and providing authoritative interpretations of Scripture and tradition helps to ensure the unity and coherence of Catholic beliefs and practices.

- **Diplomacy and International Relations:** The Vatican, as a sovereign city-state, engages in diplomatic relations with nations around the world. The Holy See, the diplomatic arm of the Vatican, maintains diplomatic missions and represents the interests of the Catholic Church on the global stage. The Pope, as the head of state of Vatican City, engages in diplomatic efforts, promotes peace and justice, and advocates for the rights and well-being of all people. The Vatican's diplomatic activities contribute to dialogue, understanding, and cooperation between the Church and other religious, political, and cultural entities.

- **Symbol of Catholic Identity:** The Vatican and the Pope serve as powerful symbols of Catholic identity and unity. They represent the historical and spiritual roots of the Church, connecting Catholics to the apostolic tradition and the early Christian community. The Vatican's grandeur, with its iconic St. Peter's Basilica and the Sistine Chapel, evokes a sense of awe and reverence, reminding Catholics of the Church's rich heritage and the universality of the faith. The Pope's presence and teachings provide a focal point for Catholics worldwide, fostering a sense of belonging and shared purpose within the global Catholic community.

The Vatican's role in governance, doctrine, diplomacy, and the preservation of Catholic identity ensures the continuity and coherence of the faith. The Pope's spiritual leadership and teachings inspire and guide Catholics worldwide, encouraging unity and shared purpose within the Church.

Chapter 4

Catholic Sacraments

T he seven sacraments are central to the Catholic faith, serving as visible signs of God's grace and presence in the lives of believers. Each sacrament is a sacred ritual that conveys specific spiritual blessings and is believed to be instituted by Jesus Christ himself.

Let's explore each sacrament:

- **Baptism:** Baptism is the first sacrament of initiation in Catholicism. Through the pouring or immersion of water and the invocation of the Holy Trinity, baptism cleanses individuals from original sin and initiates them into the Christian community. It is a rebirth into a new life in Christ and marks the beginning of one's journey as a Catholic.

- **Confirmation:** Confirmation is the sacrament in which baptized individuals receive the fullness of the Holy Spirit. Through the anointing with sacred chrism oil and the laying on of hands by a bishop, the confirmands are strengthened in their faith and receive the gifts of the Holy Spirit. Confirmation seals and completes the grace received at baptism, empowering individuals to live out their faith and witness to Christ.

- **Eucharist:** The Eucharist, also known as the Holy Communion or the Lord's Supper, is the sacrament in which Catholics receive the body and blood of Jesus Christ. During the Mass, bread and wine are consecrated by a priest, becoming the real presence of Christ. Through the reception of the Eucharist, Catholics enter into a profound union with Christ and with one another, nourishing their souls and receiving spiritual sustenance.

- **Reconciliation (Confession):** Reconciliation, also known as Confession or Penance, is the sacrament of forgiveness and reconciliation with God and the Church. Through the confession of sins to a priest, accompanied by sincere contrition and the resolution to amend one's life, Catholics receive absolution and experience God's mercy and forgiveness. Reconciliation restores the soul to a state of grace and strengthens the individual's relationship with God and the community.

- **Anointing of the Sick:** The Anointing of the Sick is the sacrament of healing and comfort for those who are seriously ill or facing the end of their earthly life. Through the anointing with holy oil and the prayers of the priest, the sick person receives spiritual and physical strength, forgiveness of sins, and the grace to face their illness with faith and hope. This sacrament brings comfort, peace, and the assurance of God's presence in times of illness and suffering.

- **Holy Orders:** Holy Orders is the sacrament through which men are ordained as deacons, priests, or bishops to serve the Church and the faithful. Through the laying on of hands by a bishop, the ordained receive a special grace and authority to preach the Gospel, celebrate the sacraments, and shepherd the people of God. Holy Orders ensures the continuation of the apostolic ministry and the pastoral care of the Church.

- **Matrimony:** Matrimony is the sacrament of marriage, in which a man and a woman enter into a lifelong covenant of love and fidelity. Through their consent and the blessing of the Church, the couple receives the grace to live out their vocation as spouses and parents. Matrimony is a sacred bond that reflects the love between Christ and the Church, and it is a source of grace and support for the couple in their journey of faith.

The seven sacraments in Catholicism are profound encounters with God's grace, providing spiritual nourishment, forgiveness, healing, and empowerment. They are visible signs of God's presence and love, inviting Catholics to deepen their relationship with God and live out their faith in the world.

Through the sacraments, Catholics are united with Christ and the Church, receiving the spiritual gifts necessary for their journey of holiness.

Significance of the Sacraments in the Life of a Catholic

The sacraments hold immense significance in the life of a Catholic. Each sacrament is a visible sign instituted by Jesus Christ himself, through which Catholics receive spiritual blessings and are united more closely with God and the Church. Let's explore that in more detail:

- **Encounter with God's Grace:** The sacraments are powerful encounters with God's grace, which is freely given to believers. Through the sacraments, Catholics receive the specific graces needed for their spiritual growth and salvation. These graces strengthen, heal, and sanctify individuals, enabling them to live out their faith more fully and to grow in holiness.

- **Union with Christ:** The sacraments unite Catholics with Jesus Christ in a profound way. In the Eucharist, Catholics receive the real presence of Christ, nourishing their souls and deepening their union with Him. Through baptism, confirmation, and the other sacraments, Catholics are incorporated into the mystical body of Christ, becoming members of His Church, and sharing in His mission.

- **Forgiveness and Reconciliation:** Several sacraments, such as reconciliation and anointing of the sick, offer forgiveness, healing, and reconciliation with God and the Church. In the sacrament of reconciliation, Catholics experience the mercy and forgiveness of God, restoring their relationship with Him and the community. The sacrament of anointing the sick brings comfort, strength, and spiritual healing to those who are ill or facing the end of their earthly life.

- **Spiritual Nourishment:** The sacraments provide spiritual nourishment for Catholics, sustaining them on their journey of faith. The Eucharist, often referred to as the "source and summit" of the Christian life, nourishes the soul with the body and blood of Christ. Through the sacraments, Catholics receive the grace and strength needed to live out their Christian vocation and to face the challenges of life with faith and hope.

- **Sacraments of Initiation:** The sacraments of initiation, namely baptism, confirmation, and the Eucharist, mark significant milestones in the life of a Catholic. Baptism initiates individuals into the Christian community, cleansing them from original sin and making them children of God. Confirmation strengthens and empowers Catholics with the gifts of the Holy Spirit. The Eucharist nourishes and sustains Catholics in their ongoing journey of faith.

- **Sacraments of Vocation:** The sacraments of matrimony and holy orders are sacraments of vocation, calling individuals to specific states of life and service within the Church. Matrimony sanctifies the marital bond, enabling couples to live out their vocation of love and self-giving. Holy orders ordain individuals as deacons, priests, or bishops, empowering them to serve the Church and the faithful.

- **Communal and Ecclesial Dimension:** The sacraments have a communal and ecclesial dimension, as they are celebrated within the context of the Church community. They foster unity among believers, as Catholics come together to participate in the sacraments and to support one another in their faith journey.

The sacraments also connect Catholics to the broader Church, both locally and globally, reinforcing their sense of belonging to the universal body of Christ.

The sacraments are transformative moments in the spiritual journey of Catholics, fostering a deeper relationship with God and a stronger sense of belonging to the Church community.

Rituals and Practices Associated With Each Sacrament

- **Baptism:** The ritual of baptism involves the pouring or immersion of water on the person's head while the priest or deacon invokes the Holy Trinity. This act symbolizes the cleansing of original sin and the initiation into the Christian community. The person being baptized, or their parents and godparents in the case of infant baptism, make promises to renounce sin and profess faith in Jesus Christ.

- **Confirmation:** The sacrament of confirmation involves the anointing with sacred chrism oil and the laying on of hands by a bishop. This ritual signifies the outpouring of the Holy Spirit upon the confirmed individual, strengthening their faith and empowering them to live as witnesses of Christ. The confirmed person may choose a saint's name as a sign of their commitment to follow in the footsteps of the saints.

- **Eucharist:** The ritual of the Eucharist, also known as the Mass or Holy Communion, involves the consecration of bread and wine by a priest during the Liturgy of the Eucharist. Catholics believe that the bread and wine become the actual body and blood of Jesus Christ while retaining the appearance of bread and wine. The faithful receive the Eucharist, consuming the consecrated host and drinking from the chalice, as a means of uniting themselves with Christ and the community of believers.

- **Reconciliation (Confession):** The ritual of reconciliation, also known as confession or penance, involves the confession of sins to a priest. The penitent expresses contrition for their sins and receives absolution, a prayer of forgiveness, from the priest. The priest may offer guidance and counsel to help the penitent grow in their spiritual life and avoid sin in the future.

- **Anointing of the Sick:** The ritual of the anointing of the sick involves the anointing with holy oil and the prayers of a priest. This sacrament is administered to those who are seriously ill or facing the end of their earthly life. The priest anoints the person's forehead and hands, invoking God's healing and comfort. The sacrament brings spiritual strength, forgiveness of sins, and the grace to face illness or suffering with faith and hope.

- **Holy Orders:** The ritual of holy orders involves the laying on of hands by a bishop upon those being ordained as deacons, priests, or bishops. The specific rituals vary depending on the level of ordination. Deacons receive the Book of the Gospels, priests receive the chalice and paten, and bishops receive the miter, crosier, and pallium. The ordination ceremony includes prayers, the recitation of vows, and the imposition of hands by the bishop and other priests.

- **Matrimony:** The ritual of matrimony involves the exchange of vows and rings between a man and a woman in the presence of a priest or deacon and witnesses. The couple makes a lifelong commitment to love, honor, and support each other, following the teachings of the Church. The priest or deacon blesses the couple, and the community offers prayers and support for their union.

These rituals and practices associated with each sacrament are essential components of the Catholic faith.

CHAPTER 5

Catholic Beliefs and Doctrines

C atholicism, as a major branch of Christianity, is built upon a foundation of core beliefs that shape the faith and guide the lives of its followers. These beliefs encompass the nature of God, the means of salvation, and the understanding of the afterlife. Understanding these core beliefs provides insight into the theological framework of Catholicism.

- **The Holy Trinity:** Central to Catholicism is the belief in the Holy Trinity. Catholics believe in one God who exists in three distinct persons: the Father, the Son (Jesus Christ), and the Holy Spirit. This belief reflects the mystery of God's nature and underscores the unity and diversity within the divine. The Trinity is seen as a community of love, and Catholics are called to participate in this divine love through their relationships with God and one another.

- **Salvation Through Jesus Christ:** Catholics believe in the redemptive work of Jesus Christ, who, through his life, death, and resurrection, offers salvation to humanity. Jesus is seen as the Son of God who became incarnate, lived a sinless life, and sacrificed himself on the cross for the forgiveness of sins. Through faith in Christ and participation in the sacraments, particularly baptism and the Eucharist, Catholics receive God's grace and are reconciled with God, leading to salvation.

- **The Afterlife:** Catholicism teaches that human beings have an immortal soul that continues to exist after death. Catholics believe in the resurrection of the body, anticipating a future bodily resurrection at the end of time. The afterlife is understood as a state of eternal communion with God, either in heaven, purgatory, or hell. Heaven is the ultimate goal, where the faithful experience the fullness of God's presence and eternal joy. Purgatory is seen as a temporary state of purification for those who die in a state of grace but still require purification before entering heaven. Hell is understood as the state of eternal separation from God for those who die in a state of mortal sin and reject God's love.

The Role of Tradition, Scripture, and Magisterium in Catholic Theology

Catholic theology is shaped by a dynamic interplay between tradition, scripture, and the magisterium. These three pillars provide a comprehensive framework for understanding and interpreting the teachings of the Catholic Church. Each element contributes to the formation of doctrine, the preservation of truth, and the guidance of the faithful.

Understanding the role of tradition, scripture, and magisterium in Catholic theology is essential for comprehending the richness and complexity of the Catholic faith.

- **Tradition:** Tradition, also known as Sacred Tradition, refers to the living transmission of the teachings, practices, and beliefs of the early Christian community. It encompasses the oral teachings of Jesus and the apostles, as well as the subsequent development and interpretation of these teachings by the early Church Fathers and subsequent generations. Tradition is seen as a source of divine revelation, alongside scripture, and is considered authoritative in Catholic theology. It provides a continuity of faith and ensures the preservation of essential truths and practices throughout history. Tradition is expressed in various forms, including liturgy, prayers, devotions, theological writings, and the teachings of the Church Fathers.

- **Scripture:** Scripture, specifically the Bible, holds a central place in Catholic theology. The Bible is considered the inspired Word of God and is seen as a primary source of divine revelation. The Catholic Church recognizes both the Old Testament and the New Testament as sacred scripture. The Bible is interpreted within the context of tradition and guided by the magisterium to ensure a faithful understanding of its teachings. The interpretation of scripture is approached through various methods, including historical, literary, and theological analysis. The study of scripture is encouraged among Catholics to deepen their understanding of God's revelation and to apply its teachings to their lives.

- **Magisterium:** The magisterium refers to the teaching authority of the Catholic Church, exercised by the Pope and the bishops in communion with him. The magisterium is responsible for preserving, interpreting, and transmitting the deposit of faith, which includes both scripture and tradition. It ensures the fidelity and unity of Catholic doctrine and provides authoritative guidance on matters of faith and morals. The magisterium is guided by the Holy Spirit and is considered infallible when teaching on matters of faith and morals ex cathedra (from the chair of Peter). The magisterium is expressed through various means, including papal encyclicals, apostolic exhortations, and official documents issued by the Vatican.

It is important to note that tradition, scripture, and magisterium are not seen as separate or conflicting sources, but rather as interconnected and mutually enriching. They work together to safeguard the integrity of the faith, ensuring that the teachings of the Catholic Church remain rooted in the apostolic tradition and responsive to the needs of the faithful.

The interplay between tradition, scripture, and magisterium provides a dynamic and living theology that continues to evolve while remaining faithful to the deposit of faith entrusted to the Church.

Controversial Doctrines and Their Interpretations

Catholic theology encompasses a wide range of doctrines that have been the subject of debate and controversy throughout history. These controversial doctrines often arise from complex theological concepts and interpretations of scripture and tradition.

While the Catholic Church maintains its authoritative stance on these doctrines, there may be differing interpretations and understandings among theologians and the faithful. Exploring these controversial doctrines and their interpretations provides insight into the diversity of thought within Catholic theology.

- **Papal Infallibility:** One controversial doctrine is papal infallibility, which asserts that the Pope is preserved from error when speaking ex cathedra (from the chair of Peter) on matters of faith and morals. This doctrine was formally defined at the First Vatican Council in 1870. Some interpret this doctrine narrowly, applying it only to a limited number of papal pronouncements, while others interpret it more broadly, extending it to a wider range of teachings. Controversies surrounding papal infallibility often revolve around the extent of the Pope's authority and the criteria for infallible pronouncements.

- **Contraception:** The Catholic Church teaches that the use of artificial contraception is morally wrong. This teaching is based on the belief that sexual acts should be open to the possibility of procreation and that the deliberate frustration of this purpose is contrary to God's plan for human sexuality. However, there are differing interpretations and understandings among Catholics regarding the moral implications of contraception. Some argue for a more flexible approach, taking into account the circumstances and intentions of individuals, while others adhere strictly to the Church's teaching.

- **Homosexuality:** The Catholic Church teaches that homosexual acts are morally disordered, as they are seen as contrary to the natural law and the purpose of human sexuality. However, the Church also teaches that individuals with same-sex attraction should be treated with respect, compassion, and sensitivity. There are ongoing debates and discussions within Catholic theology regarding the pastoral care and inclusion of LGBTQ+ individuals in the Church. Some theologians advocate for a more inclusive approach, emphasizing the importance of love, acceptance, and pastoral support for LGBTQ+ individuals, while others maintain a more traditional stance.

- **Women's Ordination:** The Catholic Church teaches that only men can be ordained as priests, based on the understanding that Jesus chose only men as his apostles. This teaching has been a subject of controversy and debate, with some advocating for the ordination of women to the priesthood, citing principles of equality and justice. Others argue for the preservation of the Church's tradition and the theological significance of the male priesthood. The question of women's ordination continues to be a topic of discussion within Catholic theology.

- **Divorce and Remarriage:** The Catholic Church upholds the indissolubility of marriage, teaching that a valid sacramental marriage cannot be dissolved by any human authority. Divorce and remarriage without an annulment are considered to be contrary to the teachings of the Church. However, there are differing interpretations and pastoral practices regarding the pastoral care of divorced and remarried Catholics. Some advocate for a more compassionate and inclusive approach, emphasizing the importance of mercy and pastoral discernment, while others maintain a stricter interpretation of the Church's teachings.

CHAPTER 6

Liturgical Calendar and Worship

The liturgical year is a central aspect of Catholic worship, providing a structured framework for the celebration of key events and mysteries of the faith. It is a cyclical calendar that guides the rhythm of Catholic liturgical life, marking the seasons, feasts, and solemnities that commemorate the life, death, and resurrection of Jesus Christ.

- **Advent:** The liturgical year begins with the season of Advent, a period of preparation and anticipation for the coming of Christ. It lasts for four weeks and focuses on themes of hope, expectation, and repentance. Advent is a time of spiritual reflection and preparation for the celebration of Christmas.

- **Christmas:** The Christmas season celebrates the birth of Jesus Christ. It begins with the vigil Mass on Christmas Eve and continues for twelve days, culminating in the feast of the Epiphany. During this season, Catholics reflect on the mystery of the Incarnation and the significance of Christ's birth for humanity.

- **Ordinary Time:** Following the Christmas season, the liturgical year enters a period known as Ordinary Time. This is a time of growth and discipleship, marked by the color green, which symbolizes hope and life. Ordinary Time is divided into two parts: the first occurring between Christmas and Lent, and the second between Pentecost and Advent.

- **Lent:** Lent is a season of penance, reflection, and preparation for Easter. It lasts for forty days, symbolizing the forty days

Jesus spent in the desert. Catholics are called to prayer, fasting, and almsgiving during this time, as they seek to deepen their relationship with God and prepare for the celebration of Christ's passion, death, and resurrection.

- **Easter Triduum:** The Easter Triduum is the highlight of the liturgical year, encompassing Holy Thursday, Good Friday, and the Easter Vigil. It commemorates the passion, death, and resurrection of Jesus Christ. The Triduum begins with the Mass of the Lord's Supper on Holy Thursday, continues with the veneration of the Cross on Good Friday, and culminates in the Easter Vigil, where the resurrection of Christ is celebrated.

- **Easter Season:** The Easter season follows the Easter Vigil and lasts for fifty days, concluding with the feast of Pentecost. It is a time of joy and celebration, as Catholics reflect on the resurrection of Christ and the victory over sin and death. The Easter season is marked by the color white, symbolizing purity, and new life.

- **Pentecost:** Pentecost marks the descent of the Holy Spirit upon the apostles, empowering them to spread the Gospel. It is considered the birthday of the Church. Pentecost is a time of renewal and the celebration of the Holy Spirit's presence and guidance in the life of the Church.

Throughout the liturgical year, various feasts, solemnities, and memorials are celebrated, honoring saints, events in the life of Christ, and important moments in salvation history. These include the feasts of the Annunciation, the Assumption of Mary, All Saints' Day, and the feast of Christ the King, among others.

The liturgical year provides a structured and meaningful way for Catholics to engage in worship, prayer, and reflection. It invites the faithful to journey through the mysteries of Christ's life, death, and resurrection, deepening their understanding of the faith and fostering a closer relationship with God.

Major Feasts, Seasons, and Celebrations

Catholicism is rich in feasts, seasons, and celebrations that mark significant events and mysteries of the faith. These observances provide opportunities for Catholics to deepen their spiritual journey, reflect on the life of Christ, honor saints, and engage in communal worship.

Let's explore some of the major feasts, seasons, and celebrations in Catholicism to offer insight into the diverse and vibrant liturgical life of the Church.

- **Christmas:** Christmas is one of the most important feasts in Catholicism, celebrating the birth of Jesus Christ. It is observed on December 25th and is preceded by the season of Advent, a time of preparation and anticipation. Christmas is marked by joyful liturgies, the Nativity scene, carol singing, and the exchange of gifts. The celebration continues for twelve days, culminating in the feast of the Epiphany, which commemorates the visit of the Magi to the infant Jesus.

- **Easter:** Easter is the most significant feast in the liturgical year, celebrating the resurrection of Jesus Christ. It is preceded by the season of Lent, a period of penance and preparation. Easter Sunday, also known as Resurrection Sunday, is the pinnacle of the Easter celebration. It is marked by joyful liturgies, the lighting of the Paschal candle, the proclamation of the Easter Vigil, and the joyful proclamation, "Christ is risen!" The Easter season lasts for fifty days, concluding with the feast of Pentecost.

- **Ash Wednesday and Lent:** Ash Wednesday marks the beginning of the season of Lent, a forty-day period of fasting, prayer, and penance leading up to Easter. On Ash Wednesday, Catholics receive ashes on their foreheads as a sign of repentance and mortality. During Lent, Catholics engage in acts of self-denial, increased prayer, and works of charity. The season of

Lent invites believers to reflect on Christ's sacrifice and prepare their hearts for the celebration of Easter.

- **Pentecost:** Pentecost commemorates the descent of the Holy Spirit upon the apostles, empowering them to spread the Gospel. It is celebrated fifty days after Easter and marks the birth of the Church. Pentecost is a joyful feast, often marked by the wearing of red vestments, symbolizing the fire of the Holy Spirit. It is a time to reflect on the presence and work of the Holy Spirit in the life of the Church and to renew one's commitment to living out the faith.

- **All Saints' Day and All Souls' Day:** All Saints' Day, observed on November 1st, honors all the saints, known and unknown, who have attained heaven. It is a day to celebrate the communion of saints and to seek their intercession. All Souls' Day, observed on November 2nd, is a day to remember and pray for all the faithful departed. Catholics visit cemeteries, offer prayers, and remember their loved ones who have passed away.

- **Feast of the Assumption:** The Feast of the Assumption, celebrated on August 15th, commemorates the belief that Mary, the mother of Jesus, was assumed body and soul into heaven at the end of her earthly life. It is a day to honor Mary's unique role in salvation history and to reflect on the hope of the resurrection and the promise of eternal life.

- **Feast of Corpus Christi:** The Feast of Corpus Christi, also known as the Solemnity of the Most Holy Body and Blood of Christ, celebrates the real presence of Jesus Christ in the Eucharist. It is observed on the Thursday after Trinity Sunday, which falls on the eighth Sunday after Easter. The feast includes processions, adoration of the Blessed Sacrament, and special liturgies that highlight the significance of the Eucharist in Catholic worship.

These major feasts, seasons, and celebrations in Catholicism provide opportunities for believers to engage in communal worship, deepen their understanding of the faith, and celebrate the mysteries of Christ's life, death, and resurrection.

Structure of Catholic Mass and Other Forms of Worship

The structure of the Catholic Mass and other forms of worship in Catholicism follow a well-defined pattern that reflects the rich liturgical tradition of the Church. The Mass, which is the central act of Catholic worship, is characterized by its order, symbolism, and reverence.

In this section, we will explore the structure of the Mass and other forms of worship provides insight into the significance and purpose of each element, fostering a deeper appreciation for the Catholic liturgical tradition.

- **Introductory Rites:** The Mass begins with the introductory rites, which include the entrance procession, the sign of the cross, the greeting, and the penitential rite. These rites serve to gather the faithful, prepare their hearts for worship, and acknowledge their need for God's mercy and forgiveness.

- **Liturgy of the Word:** The Liturgy of the Word is a central part of the Mass, during which the Scriptures are proclaimed and reflected upon. It typically includes readings from the Old Testament, the Psalms, the New Testament Epistles, and the Gospel. The readings are followed by a homily, in which the priest or deacon offers a reflection on the Word of God. The congregation responds with the recitation of the Creed, professing their faith.

- **Liturgy of the Eucharist:** The Liturgy of the Eucharist is the high point of the Mass, during which the bread and wine are consecrated and become the body and blood of Jesus Christ. This part of the Mass includes the presentation of the gifts, the Eucharistic prayer, the Lord's Prayer, the sign of peace, and the reception of Holy Communion. The faithful partake in the Eucharist, receiving the body and blood of Christ as a means of spiritual nourishment and unity with God and one another.

- **Concluding Rites:** The Mass concludes with the concluding rites, which include the final blessing, the dismissal, and the recessional hymn. The priest or deacon sends forth the congregation to go forth and live out their faith in the world, carrying the grace and blessings received during the Mass.

In addition to the Mass, there are other forms of worship in Catholicism that follow a similar structure and incorporate various devotions and practices. These include:

- **Liturgy of the Hours:** The Liturgy of the Hours, also known as the Divine Office, is a form of prayer that consists of psalms, readings, and prayers offered at specific times throughout the day. It is a way for the faithful to sanctify the day and join in the Church's continuous prayer.

- **Sacraments:** The celebration of the sacraments, such as baptism, confirmation, reconciliation, anointing of the sick, matrimony, and holy orders, follows a specific liturgical structure. Each sacrament has its own rituals, prayers, and gestures that reflect its unique significance and purpose.

- **Devotions:** Devotions, such as the Rosary, Stations of the Cross, novenas, and adoration of the Blessed Sacrament, are additional forms of worship in Catholicism. These devotions provide opportunities for personal prayer, reflection, and deepening of one's relationship with God and the saints.

- **Feast Days and Solemnities:** Throughout the liturgical year, the Church celebrates various feast days and solemnities that commemorate significant events and individuals in the life of Christ and the saints. These celebrations often include special liturgies, processions, and devotions that highlight the particular theme or mystery being commemorated.

The structure of Catholic Mass and other forms of worship is designed to facilitate active participation, reverence, and encounter with the divine. It provides a framework for the faithful to engage in communal prayer, receive the sacraments, and deepen their relationship with God.

CHAPTER 7

Catholic Moral Teachings

C atholicism places a strong emphasis on ethical principles and moral teachings. These principles and teachings serve as a guide for Catholics in their daily lives, helping them make decisions that align with their faith and contribute to the greater good.

Let's explore some of the key ethical principles and moral teachings in Catholicism.

- **Dignity of the Human Person:** Catholicism teaches that every human being is created in the image and likeness of God, and therefore possesses inherent dignity and worth. This principle emphasizes the respect and protection of human life from conception to natural death. It forms the basis for Catholic teachings on issues such as abortion, euthanasia, and capital punishment.

- **Common Good:** The Catholic Church teaches that individuals are part of a larger community and have a responsibility to work towards the common good. This principle emphasizes the importance of promoting social justice, solidarity, and the well-being of all members of society. It calls for Catholics to actively engage in efforts to alleviate poverty, promote equality, and address systemic injustices.

- **Solidarity:** Solidarity is a core principle in Catholic social teaching. It emphasizes the interconnectedness of all people and calls for a sense of unity and shared responsibility. Catholics are encouraged to stand in solidarity with the poor, marginalized, and oppressed, advocating for their rights, and working towards a more just and equitable society.

- **Subsidiarity:** Subsidiarity is the principle that decisions should be made at the most local level possible, allowing individuals and communities to have a say in matters that affect them directly. This principle promotes the empowerment of individuals and communities, recognizing their autonomy and capacity to make decisions for themselves.

- **Stewardship of Creation:** Catholicism teaches that human beings have a responsibility to care for and protect the environment, as it is a gift from God. This principle calls for responsible and sustainable use of natural resources, as well as efforts to address climate change and preserve biodiversity.

- **Virtues and Moral Life:** Catholicism places a strong emphasis on cultivating virtues and living a moral life. Virtues such as love, justice, honesty, humility, and compassion are seen as essential for personal growth and building healthy relationships. Catholics are encouraged to develop these virtues through prayer, reflection, and the sacraments, and to apply them in their interactions with others.

- **Sacraments and Moral Formation:** The sacraments, such as baptism, Eucharist, and reconciliation, play a significant role in Catholic moral formation. They provide opportunities for individuals to receive grace, seek forgiveness, and strengthen their commitment to living a moral life. The sacraments are seen as transformative experiences that deepen one's relationship with God and empower individuals to live out their faith in the world.

It is important to note that Catholic ethical principles and moral teachings are not static but evolve over time in response to new challenges and societal changes. The Catholic Church, through its teachings and guidance, seeks to provide a moral compass for its followers, helping them navigate the complexities of the modern world while remaining rooted in their faith.

Societal Issues and Bioethics From a Catholic Perspective

From a Catholic perspective, issues such as social justice, human rights, and bioethics are of great importance. The Catholic Church has a long-standing tradition of advocating for the dignity and well-being of all individuals, and these issues are seen as integral to the promotion of a just and compassionate society.

Let's delve into each of these topics in more detail.

- **Social Justice:** Social justice is a central theme in Catholic social teaching. It emphasizes the fair distribution of resources, equal opportunities, and the eradication of systemic injustices. The Catholic Church teaches that all individuals have a right to the basic necessities of life, such as food, shelter, healthcare, and education. It calls for the elimination of poverty, discrimination, and oppression, and encourages Catholics to actively engage in efforts to promote social justice. This includes advocating for policies that address income inequality, supporting initiatives that empower marginalized communities, and working towards the common good.

- **Human Rights:** Catholicism upholds the inherent dignity and worth of every human being, and therefore recognizes the importance of protecting and promoting human rights. The Catholic Church teaches that human rights are rooted in the belief that all individuals are created in the image and likeness of God. This includes the right to life, freedom of conscience and religion, freedom from torture and slavery, and the right to participate in society. Catholics are called to respect and defend these rights, both in their personal lives and in society at large. This involves speaking out against human rights abuses, supporting organizations that promote human rights, and working towards the establishment of just laws and policies.

- **Bioethics:** Bioethics refers to the ethical considerations surrounding issues related to human life and health, such as abortion, euthanasia, genetic engineering, and medical research. From a Catholic perspective, human life is sacred and should be protected from conception to natural death. The Catholic Church teaches that all human beings, regardless of their stage of development or health condition, have an inherent dignity and right to life. Therefore, practices such as abortion and euthanasia are considered morally wrong. Additionally, the Catholic Church promotes ethical guidelines for medical research and technology, emphasizing the importance of respecting human dignity, informed consent, and the common good.

In addressing these issues, the Catholic Church draws upon its rich theological and moral tradition, as well as the teachings of Scripture and the guidance of the Magisterium (the teaching authority of the Church). It encourages Catholics to engage in dialogue, reflection, and prayer to discern the best ways to address these complex issues in light of their faith.

It is important to note that while the Catholic Church provides guidance on these issues, individual Catholics may have differing perspectives and interpretations. The Church encourages respectful dialogue and the formation of conscience, recognizing that individuals may have different experiences and insights that contribute to the ongoing exploration of these topics.

In summary, from a Catholic perspective, social justice, human rights, and bioethics are seen as integral to the promotion of a just and compassionate society. The Catholic Church calls upon its followers to actively engage in efforts to address these issues, guided by the principles of human dignity, solidarity, and the common good.

Application of Catholic Moral Teachings in Everyday Life

Catholic moral teachings provide a framework for making ethical decisions and navigating the complexities of the modern world. Let's explore how these teachings can be applied in various aspects of everyday life.

- **Personal Relationships:** Catholic moral teachings emphasize the importance of love, respect, and compassion in personal relationships. This includes treating others with kindness and dignity, practicing forgiveness, and fostering healthy communication. Catholics are called to prioritize the well-being of others, seeking to build strong and nurturing relationships based on mutual respect and care.

- **Work and Professional Life:** Catholic moral teachings extend to the realm of work and professional life. Catholics are encouraged to approach their work with integrity, honesty, and a commitment to the common good. This involves treating colleagues and employees fairly, respecting the rights and dignity of all individuals, and striving for excellence in one's professional endeavors. Additionally, Catholic social teaching emphasizes the importance of just wages, safe working conditions, and the protection of workers' rights.

- **Social Justice and Advocacy:** Catholic moral teachings place a strong emphasis on social justice and advocacy for the marginalized and vulnerable. Catholics are called to actively engage in efforts to address systemic injustices, alleviate poverty, and promote equality. This can involve volunteering with organizations that serve the poor, advocating for policies that promote social justice, and raising awareness about issues such as racism, immigration, and environmental stewardship.

- **Ethical Consumption:** Catholic moral teachings encourage responsible and ethical consumption. This includes being mindful of the impact of one's purchasing choices on the environment, supporting fair trade practices, and avoiding products that are produced through exploitative labor or harm the common good. Catholics are called to be good stewards of the Earth and to consider the ethical implications of their consumption habits.

- **Bioethics and Healthcare:** Catholic moral teachings provide guidance on ethical considerations in healthcare and bioethics. This includes respecting the sanctity of human life from conception to natural death, advocating for the rights of the unborn, and promoting ethical practices in medical research and treatment. Catholics are called to uphold the dignity and worth of every human being, and to make decisions regarding healthcare that align with these principles.

- **Civic Engagement:** Catholic moral teachings encourage active civic engagement and responsible citizenship. This involves participating in the democratic process, advocating for policies that promote the common good, and working towards the betterment of society. Catholics are called to be voices for justice and to use their influence to create positive change in their communities.

It is important to note that the applying moral teachings in everyday life is a lifelong journey that requires ongoing reflection, discernment, and growth. Catholics are encouraged to seek guidance from Scripture, the teachings of the Church, and the wisdom of spiritual mentors. Additionally, the sacraments, prayer, and participation in the faith community provide nourishment and support in living out these moral teachings.

CHAPTER 8

Devotional Practices
and Popular Piety

P rayer, meditation, and devotional practices hold a significant place in Catholic spirituality. These practices serve as a means of deepening one's relationship with God, fostering spiritual growth, and nurturing a sense of connection to the divine.

In this section, we will explore the importance of prayer, meditation, and devotional practices in Catholic spirituality in more detail.

- **Prayer:** Prayer is a central aspect of Catholic spirituality. It is a way of communicating with God, expressing gratitude, seeking guidance, and offering praise. Through prayer, Catholics cultivate a personal relationship with God, acknowledging His presence in their lives and opening themselves to His grace. Prayer can take various forms, including vocal prayers (such as the Our Father or the Hail Mary), spontaneous prayers, and contemplative prayer. It can be done individually or in community, and it can be practiced at any time and in any place. Prayer provides a space for reflection, surrender, and communion with the divine.

- **Meditation:** Meditation is a practice that involves quieting the mind, focusing one's attention, and entering into a state of deep contemplation. In Catholic spirituality, meditation is often used as a means of deepening one's understanding of Scripture, reflecting on the life and teachings of Jesus, and seeking spiritual insights. Through meditation, Catholics strive to quiet the distractions of the world and open themselves to the presence of God. This practice can involve repetitive prayers, visualizations, or simply sitting in silence and being present to the divine presence within.

- **Devotional Practices:** Devotional practices are acts of piety and devotion that are aimed at deepening one's faith and expressing love for God and the saints. These practices can include the recitation of specific prayers or devotions, such as the Rosary or the Stations of the Cross. Devotional practices often involve the use of sacred objects, such as crucifixes, icons, or statues, which serve as reminders of the divine presence. They can also include acts of service, such as caring for the poor or visiting the sick. Devotional practices provide a tangible way for Catholics to express their faith and seek spiritual nourishment.

The importance of prayer, meditation, and devotional practices in Catholic spirituality lies in their ability to foster a deeper connection with God, nourish the soul, and provide a framework for spiritual growth. These practices offer a space for reflection, self-examination, and surrender to the divine will. They provide a means of seeking guidance, finding solace in times of difficulty, and expressing gratitude for God's blessings.

Through prayer, meditation, and devotional practices, Catholics are invited to cultivate a vibrant and personal relationship with God, drawing closer to Him and aligning their lives with His will.

It is important to note that while these practices are highly valued in Catholic spirituality, they are not ends in themselves. Rather, they are means to an end—that is, deepening a relationship with God and living out the teachings of Jesus in everyday life. The ultimate goal of prayer, meditation, and devotional practices is to transform the heart and mind, leading to a life of love, compassion, and service to others.

Popular Devotions in Catholicism

Popular devotions such as the Rosary, Novenas, and pilgrimage hold a special place in Catholic spirituality. These practices have been embraced by millions of Catholics around the world as a means of deepening their faith, seeking spiritual nourishment, and expressing devotion to God and the saints.

- **The Rosary:** The Rosary is one of the most well-known and widely practiced devotions in Catholicism. It involves the recitation of prayers and meditation on the mysteries of the life, death, and resurrection of Jesus Christ and the Blessed Virgin Mary. The Rosary consists of repetitive prayers, including the Our Father, Hail Mary, and Glory Be, while meditating on specific events in the lives of Jesus and Mary. This devotion is often associated with peace, contemplation, and the intercession of the Blessed Virgin Mary. The Rosary can be prayed individually or in community, and it is often accompanied by the use of a set of beads to help keep track of the prayers.

- **Novenas:** Novenas are a form of prayer that involves nine consecutive days of focused devotion to a particular saint, event, or intention. The word "novena" comes from the Latin word "novem," meaning "nine." During a novena, Catholics engage in prayer, reflection, and acts of piety for nine days, seeking the intercession of a specific saint or asking for God's grace in a particular area of their lives. Novenas can be prayed privately or in community, and they often involve the recitation of specific prayers or devotions associated with the chosen saint or intention. Novenas are seen as a way to deepen one's relationship with God and the saints, and to seek their guidance and assistance in times of need.

- **Pilgrimage:** Pilgrimage is a practice that involves traveling to a sacred place or shrine as an act of devotion and spiritual renewal. Catholic pilgrimages can be made to sites associated with Jesus, Mary, or the saints, such as the Holy Land, Lourdes, Fatima, or the Shrine of Our Lady of Guadalupe. Pilgrims embark on these journeys with the intention of deepening their faith, seeking healing, or expressing gratitude. The physical act of pilgrimage is seen as a metaphor for the spiritual journey of the soul, and it often involves prayer, reflection, participation in liturgical celebrations, and acts of penance. Pilgrimage is considered a transformative experience that allows pilgrims to draw closer to God, seek spiritual renewal, and connect with the communion of saints.

These popular devotions hold significance in Catholic spirituality for several reasons. Firstly, they provide a tangible and accessible way for Catholics to express their faith and devotion. Through the repetition of prayers, meditation on sacred mysteries, or physical journey to a holy site, individuals can engage their senses and emotions in acts of worship and prayer. These devotions also foster a sense of community and shared faith, as many Catholics participate in these practices together, whether in their local parish or on a larger scale.

Furthermore, popular devotions serve as a means of deepening one's relationship with God and the saints. They provide opportunities for reflection, contemplation, and seeking intercession. These devotions can offer solace, guidance, and spiritual nourishment in times of difficulty or uncertainty. They also serve as a way to express gratitude, seek forgiveness, and grow in holiness.

It is important to note that while popular devotions are widely embraced and encouraged in Catholicism, they are not considered essential for salvation. They are complementary to the sacraments and the teachings of the Church, and they should always be practiced in harmony with the overall teachings and traditions of Catholic faith.

Cultural Expressions of Catholicism Around the World

Catholicism is a global religion with a rich diversity of cultural expressions. As Catholicism spread throughout the world, it encountered different cultures, traditions, and customs, resulting in a vibrant mixture of cultural expressions of the faith. These expressions encompass various aspects of Catholic life, including liturgy, art, music, architecture, festivals, and religious practices.

Let's delve into some of the cultural expressions of Catholicism seen around the world.

- **Liturgy and Worship:** The liturgy, or the public worship of the Catholic Church, is often influenced by local cultures. Different regions have developed their own unique liturgical traditions, incorporating local languages, music, and customs. For example, in Latin America, vibrant processions, colorful decorations, and lively music are often part of religious celebrations. In Africa, liturgical music and dance play a significant role in worship, reflecting the rich cultural heritage of the continent. These cultural expressions enhance the worship experience and create a sense of belonging for the local Catholic communities.

- **Art and Architecture:** Catholicism has a long history of inspiring artistic expression. Throughout the centuries, artists have created magnificent works of art and architecture to depict biblical stories, saints, and religious themes. From the grand cathedrals of Europe to the intricate carvings of African churches, the cultural diversity of Catholic art and architecture is evident. Each region has its own unique style and artistic traditions, reflecting the local culture and history. These artistic expressions serve as a visual representation of the faith and inspire awe and reverence among believers.

- **Music and Hymnody:** Music holds a special place in Catholic worship and is often influenced by local cultures. Traditional hymns, chants, and songs are sung in various languages and musical styles around the world. For example, Gregorian chant is associated with the Western tradition, while African, Latin American, and Asian cultures have their own distinct musical traditions that are incorporated into Catholic liturgy. Music is a powerful tool for expressing faith, fostering community, and creating a sense of unity among believers.

• **Festivals and Celebrations:** Catholicism is known for its vibrant festivals and celebrations, which often blend religious and cultural traditions. These events provide an opportunity for communities to come together, express their faith, and celebrate their cultural heritage. Examples include the Feast of Santo Niño in the Philippines, Carnival in Brazil, and the Holy Week processions in Spain. These festivals are marked by colorful parades, traditional costumes, music, dance, and elaborate rituals, creating a unique cultural experience that reflects the local Catholic identity.

• **Religious Practices and Customs:** Catholicism is not only a religious belief system but also a way of life that influences daily practices and customs. Different cultures have developed their own unique religious practices and customs within the framework of Catholicism. These can include pilgrimages to sacred sites, veneration of local saints, traditional prayers, and customs associated with sacraments and religious milestones. These practices reflect the cultural values, traditions, and spirituality of the local Catholic communities.

These cultural expressions are a testament to the universality of the faith and its ability to adapt and integrate with diverse cultures. These expressions enrich the Catholic experience, fostering a sense of belonging, and providing a deeper understanding of the faith. They serve as a reminder that Catholicism is not a monolithic entity but a living and dynamic faith that embraces and celebrates the cultural diversity of its followers.

CHAPTER 9

Catholicism and Ecumenism

C atholic relations with other Christian denominations have evolved significantly over the centuries. The Catholic Church recognizes the importance of fostering unity among all Christians and has made efforts to engage in dialogue, build bridges, and seek common ground with other Christian traditions.

The division between the Catholic Church and other Christian denominations can be traced back to the Great Schism of 1054, which resulted in the separation of the Eastern Orthodox Church from the Roman Catholic Church. The Protestant Reformation in the 16th century further deepened the divisions within Christianity. These historical events created theological, doctrinal, and ecclesiastical differences that have shaped the relationships between Catholicism and other Christian denominations.

In the 20th century, the ecumenical movement emerged as a response to the desire for Christian unity. The Catholic Church has actively participated in this movement, engaging in dialogue and collaboration with other Christian traditions. The Second Vatican Council (1962-1965) played a significant role in promoting ecumenism within Catholicism, emphasizing the importance of dialogue, mutual understanding, and cooperation among Christians.

Catholic relations with other Christian denominations are characterized by ongoing dialogue and efforts to find common ground. The Catholic Church has engaged in theological discussions with various Christian traditions, seeking to address doctrinal differences and promote greater understanding. These dialogues have resulted in agreements on important theological issues, such as the Joint Declaration on the Doctrine of Justification with Lutherans in 1999.

Catholicism recognizes the importance of interfaith dialogue and cooperation with other religious traditions. The Catholic Church has engaged in dialogue with non-Christian religions, seeking to promote mutual respect, understanding, and collaboration on issues of common concern, such as peace, justice, and human rights.

Despite the progress made in Catholic relations with other Christian denominations, challenges and obstacles remain. Theological differences, historical grievances, and differing ecclesiastical structures continue to pose challenges to full unity. Issues such as the nature of the Eucharist, the role of the papacy, and the interpretation of Scripture are areas of ongoing theological discussion and disagreement.

The Catholic Church has taken various initiatives to promote ecumenism and foster closer relations with other Christian denominations. These include joint worship services, shared social and charitable projects, and collaborative efforts in areas such as education, healthcare, and social justice. These initiatives aim to build trust, foster mutual respect, and promote unity among Christians.

Additionally, the Church actively participates in ecumenical organizations, such as the World Council of Churches and regional ecumenical bodies. These organizations provide platforms for dialogue, cooperation, and joint initiatives among different Christian traditions.

At a local level, Catholic parishes and communities often engage in ecumenical activities, such as joint prayer services, Bible studies, and social outreach programs. These grassroots efforts contribute to building relationships and fostering unity among Christians in their local contexts.

While challenges and differences remain, progress has been made through theological dialogue, joint initiatives, and grassroots ecumenism. The Catholic Church continues to work towards greater unity among all Christians, guided by the belief in the essential unity of the Body of Christ.

Efforts Toward Christian Unity and Interfaith Dialogue

Making an effort toward Christian unity is essential in promoting understanding, cooperation, and peace among different religious traditions. These efforts seek to bridge theological, doctrinal, and cultural differences, fostering mutual respect, collaboration, and a shared commitment to common values.

Let's explore the importance, challenges, and progress in the pursuit of Christian unity and interfaith dialogue.

- **Importance of Christian Unity:** Christian unity is rooted in the belief that all Christians are part of the Body of Christ and share a common faith in Jesus Christ. The unity of Christians is seen as a powerful witness to the world and a reflection of Jesus' prayer for his followers to be one (John 17:21). Christian unity promotes a sense of solidarity, cooperation, and shared mission in spreading the Gospel and addressing social issues. It also helps to counter divisions, misunderstandings, and conflicts that can arise from theological differences.

- **Ecumenical Movement:** The ecumenical movement emerged in the 20th century as a response to the desire for Christian unity. It seeks to promote dialogue, understanding, and cooperation among different Christian traditions. The movement emphasizes the importance of recognizing and appreciating the common elements of faith shared by all Christians, while also acknowledging and respecting the diversity of theological perspectives and practices.

- **Ecumenical Dialogue:** Ecumenical dialogue involves theological discussions and conversations between representatives of different Christian traditions. These dialogues aim to address doctrinal differences, clarify misunderstandings, and seek areas of agreement. They often focus on key theological topics such as the nature of the Church, sacraments, authority, and salvation. Through dialogue, Christians can deepen their understanding of one another's beliefs, build trust, and work toward greater unity.

- **Ecumenical Organizations:** Various organizations facilitate and coordinate ecumenical efforts at the global, regional, and local levels. The World Council of Churches (WCC) is one of the most prominent international bodies promoting Christian unity. It brings together numerous Christian traditions, fostering dialogue, joint initiatives, and advocacy on social justice issues. Regional and national ecumenical bodies also play a crucial role in promoting unity within specific contexts.

- **Challenges and Obstacles:** Efforts toward Christian unity face challenges and obstacles. Theological differences, historical divisions, and differing ecclesiastical structures can hinder progress. Cultural and linguistic barriers, as well as differing worship styles and practices, can also pose challenges. Additionally, deeply ingrained historical grievances and misunderstandings can create barriers to trust and cooperation. However, these challenges are not insurmountable, and ongoing dialogue and engagement can help to overcome them.

- **Interfaith Dialogue:** Interfaith dialogue involves conversations and cooperation between representatives of different religious traditions. It seeks to promote understanding, respect, and cooperation among people of different faiths. Interfaith dialogue recognizes the shared values and common concerns that exist across religious boundaries, fostering peaceful coexistence and collaboration on issues such as social justice, environmental stewardship, and religious freedom.

- **Interfaith Initiatives:** Interfaith initiatives involve joint projects, events, and activities that bring together people from different religious traditions. These initiatives promote dialogue, build relationships, and foster mutual understanding. They can include interfaith prayer services, educational programs, community service projects, and cultural exchanges. Interfaith initiatives contribute to building bridges of understanding and promoting peaceful coexistence in diverse societies.

- **Interreligious Organizations:** Numerous organizations and networks exist to facilitate interfaith dialogue and cooperation. These organizations provide platforms for dialogue, education, and joint initiatives among different religious traditions. They promote understanding, respect, and collaboration on global issues, fostering a sense of shared responsibility for the well-being of humanity.

Overall, the pursuit of Christian unity and interfaith dialogue is an ongoing journey that requires openness, humility, and a commitment to building bridges of understanding and cooperation.

Challenges and Opportunities in Ecumenical and Interreligious Dialogue

Ecumenical and interreligious dialogue present both challenges and opportunities in the pursuit of understanding, cooperation, and unity among different religious traditions. These dialogues aim to bridge theological, doctrinal, and cultural differences, fostering mutual respect, collaboration, and a shared commitment to common values.

Let's explore the challenges and opportunities within all of this, starting with the challenges in ecumenical dialogue.

- **Theological Differences:** The diverse theological perspectives among Christian traditions can pose challenges in finding common ground. Disagreements on issues such as sacraments, authority, and salvation require careful and respectful dialogue to foster understanding and seek areas of agreement.

- **Historical Divisions:** Historical divisions and conflicts between Christian traditions can create deep-seated grievances and mistrust. Overcoming these historical barriers requires patience, humility, and a willingness to acknowledge past wrongs and seek reconciliation.

- **Ecclesiastical Structures:** Differences in ecclesiastical structures and governance can complicate efforts towards unity. Questions of authority, hierarchy, and decision-making processes need to be addressed in a way that respects the diversity of traditions while seeking greater collaboration and cooperation.

- **Cultural and Linguistic Barriers:** Cultural and linguistic differences can hinder effective communication and understanding. Translation challenges, differing worship styles, and cultural practices require sensitivity and openness to ensure effective dialogue and mutual understanding.

Opportunities in Ecumenical Dialogue:

- **Shared Values and Beliefs:** Ecumenical dialogue provides an opportunity to recognize and appreciate the shared values and beliefs among different Christian traditions. Focusing on common elements of faith, such as the centrality of Christ, the importance of Scripture, and the call to love and serve others, can foster unity and collaboration.

- **Theological Reflection and Growth:** Engaging in ecumenical dialogue allows for theological reflection and growth. By listening to and learning from different perspectives, Christians can deepen their understanding of their own faith and gain new insights into the richness and diversity of the Christian tradition.

- **Joint Initiatives and Advocacy:** Ecumenical dialogue opens doors for joint initiatives and advocacy on social justice issues. Collaborative efforts in areas such as poverty alleviation, environmental stewardship, and peacebuilding can have a greater impact when different Christian traditions work together towards a common goal. d. Worship and Liturgical Exchange: Ecumenical dialogue provides opportunities for shared worship experiences and liturgical exchange. Joint prayer services, ecumenical worship events, and the sharing of liturgical practices can foster a sense of unity and mutual enrichment.

Challenges in Interreligious Dialogue:

- **Theological and Doctrinal Differences:** Interreligious dialogue involves engaging with different religious traditions, each with its own unique theological and doctrinal perspectives. Navigating these differences requires respectful dialogue, deep listening, and a willingness to understand and appreciate diverse beliefs and practices.

- **Cultural Sensitivity:** Interreligious dialogue requires cultural sensitivity and respect for the customs, traditions, and practices of different religious communities. Understanding and appreciating cultural contexts is essential for effective dialogue and building relationships.

- **Addressing Sensitive Topics:** Interreligious dialogue may involve addressing sensitive topics, such as religious exclusivity, religious pluralism, and social issues with religious implications. These discussions require a delicate balance of openness, respect, and a commitment to finding common ground while acknowledging differences.

- **Overcoming Prejudice and Stereotypes:** Interreligious dialogue challenges individuals to confront their own prejudices, stereotypes, and biases. It requires a willingness to listen, learn, and challenge preconceived notions about other religious traditions.

Opportunities in Interreligious Dialogue:

- **Mutual Understanding and Respect:** Interreligious dialogue provides an opportunity to foster mutual understanding and respect among different religious traditions. By engaging in dialogue, individuals can gain insights into the beliefs, practices, and values of others, promoting empathy and appreciation for diverse religious perspectives.

- **Collaboration on Shared Concerns:** Interreligious dialogue allows for collaboration on shared concerns, such as social justice, peacebuilding, and environmental stewardship. By working together, religious communities can address common challenges and contribute to the well-being of society.

- **Interfaith Education and Learning:** Interreligious dialogue offers opportunities for interfaith education and learning. By engaging in dialogue, individuals can deepen their knowledge of different religious traditions, dispel misconceptions, and promote religious literacy.

- **Building Relationships and Trust:** Interreligious dialogue fosters the building of relationships and trust among individuals from different religious traditions. These relationships provide a foundation for ongoing dialogue, cooperation, and friendship.

In summary, ecumenical, and interreligious dialogue present both challenges and opportunities. However, the opportunities for shared values, theological growth, joint initiatives, and mutual understanding make these dialogues essential for fostering unity, cooperation, and peace among different religious traditions.

CHAPTER 10

Catholicism and Social Justice

C atholic social teachings provide a moral framework for addressing issues such as poverty, inequality, and human rights. Rooted in the belief in the inherent dignity of every human person, these teachings call for a just and compassionate society that upholds the rights and well-being of all individuals.

Let's explore the key principles and perspectives of Catholic social teachings on these important issues.

- **Poverty:** Catholic social teachings emphasize the need to address poverty and promote economic justice. The principle of the preferential option for the poor calls for a special concern for those who are marginalized and economically disadvantaged. The Catholic Church teaches that poverty is not just a lack of material resources but also a denial of basic human rights and dignity. Catholics are called to work toward the eradication of poverty through efforts such as providing access to education, healthcare, and employment opportunities, as well as advocating for just economic policies and fair distribution of resources.

- **Inequality:** Catholic social teachings critique social and economic structures that perpetuate inequality. The principle of the common good emphasizes the importance of promoting the well-being of all members of society, particularly the most vulnerable. The Catholic Church teaches that unjust social and economic systems that concentrate wealth and power in the hands of a few are contrary to the principles of justice and solidarity. Catholics are called to work towards a more equitable society by advocating for policies that address income inequality, promote fair wages, and ensure access to basic necessities for all.

- **Human Rights:** Catholic social teachings affirm the inherent dignity and worth of every human person, and therefore emphasize the protection and promotion of human rights. The Catholic Church teaches that human rights are rooted in the belief that all individuals are created in the image and likeness of God. This includes the right to life, freedom of conscience and religion, freedom from torture and slavery, and the right to participate in society. Catholics are called to respect and defend these rights, both in their personal lives and in society at large. This involves speaking out against human rights abuses, supporting organizations that promote human rights, and working towards the establishment of just laws and policies.

- **Solidarity:** Solidarity is a core principle in Catholic social teachings. It emphasizes the interconnectedness of all people and calls for a sense of unity and shared responsibility. Catholics are encouraged to stand in solidarity with the poor, marginalized, and oppressed, advocating for their rights, and working towards a more just and equitable society. Solidarity involves recognizing that the well-being of one person or group is intimately connected to the well-being of all, and therefore calls for a commitment to social justice and the common good.

- **Subsidiarity:** Subsidiarity is another principle in Catholic social teachings that emphasizes decision-making at the most local level possible. It recognizes the importance of empowering individuals and communities to have a say in matters that affect them directly. Subsidiarity promotes the idea that decisions should be made as close to the people as possible, allowing for greater participation and autonomy. This principle supports the idea that individuals and communities have the capacity to make decisions for themselves and should be given the opportunity to do so.

Catholic social teachings provide a moral compass for addressing issues such as poverty, inequality, and human rights. They call for a society that upholds the dignity and well-being of all individuals, particularly the most vulnerable. Catholics are called to work towards a more just and compassionate society by advocating for policies that promote economic justice, address inequality, and protect human rights. By living out these teachings, Catholics seek to create a world that reflects the values of justice, solidarity, and the common good.

Historical Involvement of the Catholic Church in Social Movements

The Catholic Church has a long history of involvement in social movements, advocating for justice, equality, and the well-being of all individuals. Throughout the centuries, the Church has played a significant role in addressing social issues, promoting human rights, and working toward a more just and compassionate society.

- **Early Christian Social Witness:** From its earliest days, the Christian community demonstrated a commitment to social justice and care for the marginalized. The early Christians were known for their acts of charity, caring for the poor, widows, and orphans. They challenged societal norms by promoting equality and inclusivity, regardless of social status or background.

- **Medieval Church and Social Welfare:** During the Middle Ages, the Catholic Church played a central role in providing social welfare. Monastic orders established hospitals, orphanages, and schools, caring for the sick, the poor, and the vulnerable. The Church also advocated for the rights of peasants and sought to alleviate their suffering.

- **Abolition of Slavery:** In the 19th century, the Catholic Church played a significant role in the abolitionist movement. Popes such as Gregory XVI and Leo XIII condemned the slave trade and the institution of slavery, calling for its abolition. Catholic religious orders, such as the Jesuits, actively worked towards the liberation of slaves and the promotion of human dignity.

- **Labor Movements and Workers' Rights:** In response to the social and economic challenges of the Industrial Revolution, the Catholic Church became involved in labor movements and the fight for workers' rights. Pope Leo XIII's encyclical Rerum Novarum (1891) addressed the rights and dignity of workers, advocating for fair wages, safe working conditions, and the right to form labor unions.

- **Civil Rights Movement:** In the 20th century, the Catholic Church played a significant role in the civil rights movement, particularly in the United States. Catholic leaders such as Archbishop Joseph Rummel of New Orleans and Archbishop Joseph Bernardin of Chicago were vocal advocates for racial equality and justice. Catholic religious orders and laypeople were actively involved in the fight against racial discrimination.

- **Social Justice and Liberation Theology:** In Latin America, the Catholic Church played a crucial role in the development of liberation theology. This theological movement emphasized the Church's commitment to social justice, the preferential option for the poor, and the transformation of oppressive social structures. Many Catholic priests, religious, and laypeople were actively involved in social movements, advocating for land reform, human rights, and the empowerment of marginalized communities.

- **Peace and Anti-War Movements:** The Catholic Church has been actively involved in peace movements and the promotion of nonviolence. Popes such as Pope John XXIII and Pope John Paul II spoke out against war, nuclear weapons, and violence. The Church has been a strong advocate for peaceful resolutions to conflicts and the promotion of a culture of peace.

- **Environmental Stewardship:** In recent years, the Catholic Church has increasingly focused on environmental issues and the need for ecological stewardship. Pope Francis's encyclical Laudato Si' (2015) called for the protection of the environment, addressing issues such as climate change, pollution, and the exploitation of natural resources. The Church has been actively involved in promoting sustainable practices and advocating for environmental justice.

While challenges and controversies have arisen throughout history, the Church's involvement in social movements continues to be an important expression of its mission to bring about a more just and compassionate society.

Contemporary Efforts Toward Social Justice and Advocacy

Contemporary efforts toward social justice and advocacy encompass a wide range of initiatives and movements aimed at addressing systemic injustices, promoting equality, and advocating for the rights and well-being of marginalized communities. In recent years, there has been a growing recognition of the need to address issues such as racial inequality, gender discrimination, economic disparities, environmental degradation, and human rights violations.

The Catholic Church has been involved in many efforts in this regard; let's explore some of the key contemporary moves toward social justice and advocacy:

- **Racial Justice Movements:** In response to systemic racism and police violence, movements such as Black Lives Matter (BLM) have gained significant momentum. These movements seek to address racial inequality, advocate for police reform, and promote social and economic justice for Black communities. They have sparked conversations about systemic racism, prompted policy changes, and raised awareness about the need for racial justice.

- **Gender Equality and LGBTQ+ Rights:** The fight for gender equality and LGBTQ+ rights has gained significant traction in recent years. Movements such as #MeToo and Time's Up have shed light on issues of sexual harassment and assault, while LGBTQ+ activists have advocated for equal rights, marriage equality, and an end to discrimination based on sexual orientation or gender identity. These movements have led to increased awareness, policy changes, and a push for greater inclusivity and acceptance.

- **Climate Justice and Environmental Activism:** The urgency of addressing climate change and environmental degradation has spurred a global movement for climate justice. Activists, such as Greta Thunberg and the Fridays for Future movement, have called for immediate action to mitigate the impacts of climate change and promote sustainable practices. Efforts towards environmental justice also seek to address the disproportionate impact of environmental issues on marginalized communities.

- **Human Rights Advocacy:** Human rights organizations and activists continue to advocate for the protection and promotion of human rights globally. They work to address issues such as freedom of speech, religious freedom, access to education and healthcare, and the rights of refugees and migrants. These efforts involve raising awareness, lobbying for policy changes, and providing support to vulnerable populations.

- **Economic Justice and Workers' Rights:** Movements and organizations focused on economic justice and workers' rights advocate for fair wages, safe working conditions, and the protection of workers' rights. They seek to address income inequality, promote fair trade practices, and advocate for policies that prioritize the well-being of workers and marginalized communities.

- **Intersectional Activism:** Intersectional activism recognizes the interconnected nature of various forms of oppression and discrimination. It seeks to address the ways in which different systems of power and privilege intersect and impact individuals and communities. Intersectional activism aims to create inclusive spaces, amplify marginalized voices, and advocate for justice across multiple dimensions of identity, including race, gender, sexuality, disability, and socioeconomic status.

- **Grassroots Organizing and Community Empowerment:** Grassroots organizations and community-led initiatives play a crucial role in advocating for social justice. These efforts focus on empowering marginalized communities, building local capacity, and addressing issues specific to their contexts. Grassroots organizing often involves community education, mobilization, and collective action to bring about change from the ground up.

Contemporary efforts toward social justice and advocacy are characterized by a diverse range of approaches, strategies, and movements. These efforts are driven by a commitment to creating a more just and equitable society, challenging systemic injustices, and advocating for the rights and well-being of all individuals and communities.

CHAPTER 11

Challenges and Controversies

The Catholic Church, like any large institution, faces a range of challenges that impact its credibility, membership, and internal dynamics. These challenges include scandals, declining membership, and internal conflicts.

It is important to acknowledge these challenges while also recognizing the ongoing efforts within the Church to address them and foster renewal. Let's examine these challenges in more detail.

- **Scandals:** The Catholic Church has faced significant scandals related to the sexual abuse of minors by clergy members. These scandals have caused immense harm to victims and their families, eroded trust in the Church, and raised questions about accountability and transparency. The Church has been working to address these issues by implementing safeguarding measures, providing support to survivors, and holding perpetrators accountable. Efforts are also being made to improve the screening and formation of clergy and to create a culture of transparency and accountability.

- **Declining Membership:** Like many religious institutions, the Catholic Church has experienced a decline in membership in some regions. Factors contributing to this decline include changing societal attitudes towards religion, secularization, and the influence of individualism. Additionally, the Church faces challenges in engaging younger generations and addressing their spiritual needs. Efforts are being made to reach out to those who have drifted away from the Church, to provide relevant and meaningful forms of worship and community, and to foster a sense of belonging and purpose.

- **Internal Conflicts:** The Catholic Church is a diverse institution with a wide range of perspectives and theological interpretations. Internal conflicts can arise from differing views on issues such as liturgy, doctrine, and social teachings. These conflicts can sometimes lead to divisions and tensions within the Church. However, the Church also recognizes the importance of dialogue, respectful disagreement, and finding common ground. Efforts are being made to foster unity, promote understanding, and encourage open dialogue on important issues.

- **Clergy Shortages:** The Catholic Church is facing a shortage of priests in many regions, which can impact the availability of pastoral care and sacraments for the faithful. Factors contributing to this shortage include declining vocations, changing societal attitudes towards religious life, and the challenges of celibacy and priestly formation. The Church is exploring various approaches to address this issue, including promoting vocations, encouraging lay involvement in pastoral ministry, and exploring the possibility of ordaining married men in certain circumstances.

- **Cultural and Societal Changes:** The Catholic Church operates within a rapidly changing cultural and societal context. It faces challenges in adapting to new technologies, addressing issues such as gender equality and LGBTQ+ rights, and engaging with diverse cultural and religious traditions. The Church is called to navigate these changes while remaining faithful to its core teachings and values, seeking to find ways to communicate its message effectively and engage with the world in a meaningful way.

In facing these challenges, the Catholic Church draws upon its rich theological tradition, the guidance of the Magisterium, and the commitment of its members. It is a dynamic institution that seeks to learn from its past, adapt to the present, and shape a future that reflects its core mission of spreading the Gospel, promoting justice, and serving the needs of all people.

Controversial Issues Within Catholicism

Controversial issues within Catholicism, such as gender equality, sexuality, and reproductive rights, have been the subject of ongoing debate and discussion within the Church. These issues touch upon deeply held beliefs, theological interpretations, and societal norms, leading to diverse perspectives and differing opinions among Catholics.

We've touched upon these briefly earlier, but in this section, let's explore them in more detail and see what the Catholic Church has done to address them:

- **Gender Equality:** The Catholic Church teaches that men and women are equal in dignity but have distinct roles and responsibilities within the family and the Church. While the Church affirms the equal worth of men and women, there are differing views on the extent to which women should be allowed to hold leadership positions within the Church. Some argue for greater inclusion of women in decision-making roles, while others emphasize the complementarity of male and female roles.

- **Sexuality:** The Catholic Church teaches that sexual activity is reserved for marriage and should be open to the possibility of procreation. This teaching is based on the belief that sex is a sacred gift and should be expressed within the context of a committed marital relationship. However, there are differing views on issues such as contraception, premarital sex, and same-sex relationships. Additionally, as expressed earlier, some Catholics advocate for a more inclusive and compassionate approach towards LGBTQ+ individuals, while others emphasize adherence to traditional teachings.

- **Reproductive Rights:** The Catholic Church teaches that all human life is sacred and should be protected from conception to natural death. This teaching informs the Church's stance on issues such as abortion, contraception, and assisted reproductive technologies. The Church opposes abortion and considers it a grave moral evil. There are differing views among Catholics on issues such as access to contraception and the use of reproductive technologies, with some advocating for a more nuanced approach that takes into account individual circumstances and the promotion of responsible parenthood.

These controversial issues within Catholicism reflect the tension between upholding traditional teachings and responding to the changing social and cultural landscape. The Church engages in ongoing dialogue and reflection on these issues, seeking to balance fidelity to its core teachings with pastoral sensitivity and a commitment to social justice.

It is important to note that while there may be differing opinions within the Catholic Church on these controversial issues, the official teachings of the Church are guided by the Magisterium, which is the teaching authority of the Church. The Magisterium provides guidance and interpretation of doctrine, and Catholics are called to respect and adhere to these teachings.

Responses and Efforts Toward Addressing Challenges

The Catholic Church has responded to the challenges posed by controversial issues such as gender equality, sexuality, and reproductive rights through various efforts aimed at fostering dialogue, promoting understanding, and addressing the needs of individuals and communities.

While there may be differing perspectives within the Church, there are ongoing initiatives and responses that seek to engage with these challenges in a thoughtful and compassionate manner. These include:

- **Dialogue and Pastoral Accompaniment:** The Catholic Church recognizes the importance of engaging in dialogue and pastoral accompaniment with individuals and communities affected by these controversial issues. This involves listening to diverse perspectives, providing support and guidance, and promoting an environment of understanding and compassion. The Church seeks to create spaces where individuals can share their experiences, ask questions, and receive pastoral care that respects their dignity and upholds the teachings of the Church.

- **Theological Reflection and Discernment:** The Catholic Church engages in ongoing theological reflection and discernment on these controversial issues. Theological scholars, bishops, and theologians explore the scriptural, doctrinal, and ethical dimensions of these topics, seeking to deepen understanding and provide guidance. This reflection takes into account the richness of the Catholic tradition, the teachings of the Magisterium, and the insights of contemporary scholarship. The Church recognizes the need for ongoing discernment and dialogue as it seeks to address these complex issues.

- **Pastoral Guidelines and Documents:** The Catholic Church has issued pastoral guidelines and documents that provide guidance on these controversial issues. These documents aim to articulate the Church's teachings, provide pastoral care, and offer practical guidance for individuals and communities. For example, the Vatican's Congregation for the Doctrine of the Faith has issued documents on topics such as gender theory, homosexuality, and reproductive technologies, seeking to provide clarity and pastoral direction within the framework of Catholic teaching.

- **Social Justice and Advocacy:** The Catholic Church is actively engaged in social justice and advocacy efforts that address the underlying causes of these challenges. The Church advocates for policies and initiatives that promote human dignity, social equality, and the well-being of all individuals. It works towards addressing the root causes of poverty, inequality, and discrimination, recognizing that these issues are interconnected with controversial topics such as gender equality and reproductive rights.

- **Education and Formation:** The Catholic Church recognizes the importance of education and formation in addressing these challenges. It provides resources, programs, and initiatives that promote understanding, foster dialogue, and deepen knowledge of Catholic teachings. This includes educational programs for individuals of all ages, catechetical materials, and initiatives that promote the formation of conscience and moral discernment.

- **Interfaith and Ecumenical Dialogue:** The Catholic Church actively engages in interfaith and ecumenical dialogue on these controversial issues. It seeks to build bridges of understanding, promote mutual respect, and find common ground with individuals and communities from different religious traditions. Through dialogue, the Church aims to foster collaboration, address shared concerns, and promote social justice and human rights.

- **Encouraging Lay Involvement:** The Catholic Church recognizes the importance of lay involvement in addressing these challenges. Laypeople are encouraged to actively participate in the life of the Church, contribute their insights and experiences, and engage in efforts to promote justice and compassion. The Church values the unique perspectives and gifts that laypeople bring to these discussions and encourages their active involvement in shaping the Church's response to these challenges.

These efforts aim to foster understanding, provide pastoral care, and address the needs of individuals and communities. While there may be differing perspectives within the Church, these responses reflect a commitment to engaging with these challenges in a manner that upholds the teachings of the Church while promoting compassion, justice, and the well-being of all individuals.

CHAPTER 12

Catholic Art,
Architecture, and Culture

L ike many other religions, Catholicism has had a profound
influence on art, architecture, and cultural expressions
throughout history. The Catholic Church has been a patron of the
arts, commissioning and supporting the creation of magnificent
works that reflect the faith, inspire devotion, and communicate
theological truths.

Let's explore the influence of Catholicism on art, architecture, and
cultural expressions in more detail:

• **Art:** Catholicism has been a major source of inspiration for
  artists throughout the centuries. From the early Christian
  catacombs to the Renaissance masterpieces and beyond, Catholic
  themes and religious iconography have been central to artistic
  expression. Paintings, sculptures, mosaics, and stained-glass
  windows have depicted biblical stories, saints, and religious
  events, serving as visual aids for worship and devotion. Catholic
  art has sought to evoke a sense of awe, reverence, and spiritual
  contemplation, inviting viewers to engage with the mysteries
  of faith.

• **Architecture:** The Catholic Church has been a significant
  patron of architectural masterpieces. Cathedrals, basilicas,
  and churches have been built as sacred spaces for worship and
  reflection. Gothic cathedrals, with their soaring spires and
  intricate stained-glass windows, aimed to inspire a sense of

transcendence and draw the faithful closer to God. Renaissance and Baroque architecture incorporated grandeur and opulence, reflecting the splendor of the divine. The design and layout of Catholic churches often reflect the liturgical traditions and rituals of the faith, creating spaces that facilitate communal worship and spiritual engagement.

• **Music:** Catholicism has had a profound influence on music, with liturgical music playing a central role in worship. Gregorian chant, polyphony, and sacred hymns have been composed and performed to enhance the liturgy and express the depths of faith. Catholic composers such as Palestrina, Bach, Mozart, and many others have created masterpieces that continue to be performed and appreciated today. Catholic liturgical music seeks to elevate the soul, inspire devotion, and facilitate a deeper connection with the divine.

• **Festivals and Celebrations:** Catholicism has given rise to vibrant festivals and celebrations that blend religious traditions with local customs and cultural expressions. Processions, parades, and religious festivals mark significant events in the liturgical calendar, such as Easter, Christmas, and the feast days of saints. These celebrations often involve music, dance, colorful costumes, and elaborate rituals, creating a unique cultural experience that reflects the local Catholic identity.

• **Literature and Poetry:** Catholicism has been a source of inspiration for literature and poetry. From Dante's Divine Comedy to the works of Flannery O'Connor and Graham Greene, Catholic themes and theological insights have been explored in various literary forms. Catholic writers have delved into questions of faith, morality, and the human condition, offering profound reflections on the mysteries of life and the divine.

Catholicism has provided a rich source of inspiration for artists, architects, musicians, writers, and performers, shaping the cultural landscape, and contributing to the collective human experience. These expressions of faith continue to resonate with believers and non-believers alike, inviting contemplation, reflection, and a deeper engagement with the mysteries of life and the divine.

Iconography and Symbolism in Catholic Art

Iconography and symbolism play a significant role in Catholic art, serving as a means of communicating theological truths, evoking devotion, and deepening spiritual contemplation. Catholic art is rich in symbols and imagery that convey religious narratives, represent saints and biblical figures, and express the mysteries of faith.

Here, we explore the importance and significance of iconography and symbolism in Catholic art in more detail:

- **Religious Narratives:** Catholic art often depicts religious narratives from the Bible, such as the life of Jesus, the Virgin Mary, and the saints. These narratives are conveyed through visual storytelling, allowing viewers to engage with the stories and teachings of the faith. Iconography and symbolism help to identify and represent specific events, characters, and themes, making the narratives accessible and relatable.

- **Representation of Saints and Biblical Figures:** Catholic art frequently portrays saints and biblical figures, using specific symbols and attributes to identify them. For example, St. Peter is often depicted with keys, symbolizing his role as the keeper of the keys to heaven, while St. Paul is shown with a sword, representing his martyrdom. These symbols help viewers identify and connect with the saints, invoking their intercession and inspiring devotion.

- **Theological Concepts and Doctrines:** Iconography and symbolism in Catholic art are used to convey theological concepts and doctrines. For example, the crucifixion scene represents the sacrifice of Jesus and the redemption of humanity. The dove symbolizes the Holy Spirit, while the lamb represents Christ's sacrificial nature. These symbols serve as visual reminders of core theological teachings, inviting viewers to reflect on the mysteries of faith.

- **Spiritual Contemplation and Meditation:** Catholic art often incorporates symbols and imagery that invite viewers to engage in spiritual contemplation and meditation. For example, the use of halos around the heads of saints signifies their holiness and divine illumination. The use of light and color can evoke a sense of transcendence and create a sacred atmosphere. These elements encourage viewers to enter into a deeper spiritual experience and connect with the divine.

- **Universal Language of Faith:** Iconography and symbolism in Catholic art serve as a universal language of faith, transcending cultural and linguistic barriers. They communicate spiritual truths and evoke emotional responses that can be understood by believers across different cultures and time periods. This universality allows Catholic art to speak to the human experience and foster a sense of unity among believers.

- **Devotional Aids:** Catholic art, particularly in the form of religious icons, serves as devotional aids. Icons are considered windows to the divine, inviting viewers to enter into a deeper relationship with God and the saints. They are used as objects of veneration, focal points for prayer, and aids in meditation. The symbols and imagery in icons help believers focus their thoughts and emotions, facilitating a deeper connection with the divine.

Iconography and symbolism are integral to Catholic art, conveying religious narratives, representing saints and biblical figures, and expressing theological concepts. They serve as visual aids for worship, evoke devotion, and deepen spiritual contemplation. Through the use of symbols and imagery, Catholic art invites viewers to engage with the mysteries of faith, fostering a deeper understanding and connection with the divine.

Preservation and Interpretation of Catholic Cultural Heritage

The preservation and interpretation of Catholic cultural heritage is of great importance in ensuring the continuity and understanding of the rich artistic, architectural, and cultural legacy of the Catholic Church. It involves efforts to safeguard and promote the tangible and intangible aspects of Catholic heritage, including artworks, historical sites, liturgical practices, and traditions.

- **Conservation and Restoration:** Preservation efforts involve the conservation and restoration of artworks, artifacts, and historical sites associated with Catholicism. This includes the careful maintenance, repair, and protection of physical structures, paintings, sculptures, manuscripts, and other cultural artifacts. Conservation experts employ scientific techniques and ethical principles to ensure the longevity and authenticity of these treasures, allowing future generations to appreciate and learn from them.

- **Documentation and Archiving: The** documentation and archiving of Catholic cultural heritage are crucial for its preservation and interpretation. This involves the systematic recording and cataloging of artworks, historical documents, photographs, and other relevant materials. Digital technologies are increasingly used to create comprehensive databases and virtual archives, making these resources accessible to researchers, scholars, and the general public.

- **Museums and Exhibitions:** Museums and exhibitions play a vital role in the interpretation and presentation of Catholic cultural heritage. They provide spaces for the display and contextualization of artworks, artifacts, and historical objects. Museums often employ curators, educators, and researchers who engage in scholarly research, develop interpretive materials, and design exhibitions that convey the historical, artistic, and spiritual significance of Catholic heritage.

- **Educational Programs and Outreach:** Educational programs and outreach initiatives are essential for the interpretation and dissemination of Catholic cultural heritage. These programs aim to engage diverse audiences, including students, scholars, tourists, and the local community. They may include guided tours, lectures, workshops, and interactive activities that promote a deeper understanding and appreciation of Catholic art, architecture, and traditions.

- **Liturgical Practices and Rituals:** The preservation and interpretation of Catholic cultural heritage extend to liturgical practices and rituals. These practices, such as the celebration of the Mass, sacraments, and devotions, are deeply rooted in tradition and carry significant historical and spiritual meaning. Efforts are made to ensure the continuity and authenticity of these practices while also allowing for contextual adaptations that respect cultural diversity and promote active participation.

- **Cultural Tourism and Pilgrimage:** Cultural tourism and pilgrimage provide opportunities for individuals to engage with Catholic cultural heritage in a meaningful way. Pilgrimage sites, such as shrines and holy places, attract visitors seeking spiritual enrichment and a connection to the historical and religious significance of these locations. Cultural tourism initiatives promote responsible and sustainable travel, encouraging visitors to appreciate and respect the cultural heritage they encounter.

- **Interdisciplinary Research and Collaboration:** The preservation and interpretation of Catholic cultural heritage benefit from interdisciplinary research and collaboration. Scholars, theologians, historians, archaeologists, art historians, and conservation experts work together to deepen our understanding of Catholic heritage, its historical context, and its theological significance. Collaboration between academic institutions, religious organizations, and cultural heritage institutions fosters a holistic approach to research, interpretation, and preservation.

These efforts ensure the continuity, understanding, and appreciation of the rich artistic, architectural, and cultural legacy of the Catholic Church. By safeguarding and interpreting Catholic cultural heritage, we can connect with the past, deepen our faith, and foster a sense of continuity and identity within the Catholic community and beyond.

CHAPTER 13

Catholic Education and Intellectual Tradition

C atholic education plays a significant role in shaping religious identity and values for individuals who are part of the Catholic faith. It provides a unique and comprehensive approach to education that integrates faith, knowledge, and moral development. The aim of Catholic education is to nurture the whole person, fostering spiritual growth, intellectual curiosity, and moral integrity.

One of the primary objectives of Catholic education is to instill a deep understanding and appreciation of Catholic teachings, traditions, and values. Through religious instruction, students are introduced to the core beliefs and principles of the Catholic Church, such as the Ten Commandments, the Beatitudes, and the sacraments. They learn about the life and teachings of Jesus Christ, the importance of prayer, and the significance of participating in the sacramental life of the Church.

Catholic schools also provide a faith-filled environment where students can actively practice their faith. Regular participation in Mass, prayer services, and religious celebrations helps students develop a personal relationship with God and fosters a sense of community and belonging. The presence of priests, religious sisters, and lay catechists within Catholic schools further strengthens the faith formation process, as they serve as role models and spiritual guides for students.

In addition to religious instruction, Catholic education places a strong emphasis on academic excellence and character development. Students are encouraged to strive for intellectual growth and to develop critical thinking skills. The integration of faith and reason allows students to see the interconnectedness of their faith with various academic disciplines, fostering a holistic understanding of the world.

Catholic schools also prioritize the development of moral values and virtues. Students are taught to live out the Gospel values of love, compassion, justice, and service to others. They are encouraged to practice kindness, respect, and empathy in their interactions with peers and the wider community. Through service projects and outreach programs, students are given opportunities to put their faith into action and make a positive difference in the world.

Furthermore, Catholic education promotes a sense of social responsibility and a commitment to social justice. Students are encouraged to be advocates for the marginalized and to work towards creating a more just and equitable society. They are taught to recognize the dignity and worth of every human person, regardless of their background or circumstances.

The role of Catholic education in shaping religious identity and values extends beyond the classroom. It involves the collaboration of parents, teachers, and the wider faith community. The partnership between home, school, and the Church creates a supportive and nurturing environment where students can grow in their faith and develop a strong moral compass.

In conclusion, Catholic education plays a vital role in shaping religious identity and values by providing a comprehensive and integrated approach to education. It fosters a deep understanding of Catholic teachings, encourages active participation in the sacramental life of the Church, promotes academic excellence, and nurtures moral and ethical development. Through the collaboration of various stakeholders, Catholic education strives to form individuals who are grounded in their faith, equipped with knowledge, and committed to making a positive impact in the world.

Contributions of Catholic Scholars and Intellectuals Throughout History

Throughout history, Catholic scholars and intellectuals have made significant contributions to various fields of knowledge, ranging from theology and philosophy to science, literature, and the arts. Their work has not only enriched the Catholic intellectual tradition but has also had a profound impact on the broader academic and cultural landscape.

In the realm of theology and philosophy, Catholic scholars have played a pivotal role in shaping religious thought and understanding. One of the most influential figures in this regard is St. Thomas Aquinas, a Dominican friar and theologian of the 13th century. Aquinas's synthesis of Christian theology with Aristotelian philosophy, known as Thomism, has had a lasting impact on Catholic theology and continues to be studied and debated to this day. His works, such as the Summa Theologica, have provided a framework for understanding the nature of God, the human person, and the relationship between faith and reason.

Another notable Catholic scholar is St. Augustine of Hippo, whose writings on theology and philosophy have had a profound influence on Western thought. Augustine's exploration of topics such as original sin, grace, and the nature of evil has shaped Christian theology and has been a source of inspiration for countless theologians and philosophers throughout the centuries.

In the field of science, Catholic scholars have made significant contributions that have advanced our understanding of the natural world. One such example is the Belgian priest and physicist Georges Lemaître, who proposed the theory of the Big Bang, which is now widely accepted as the explanation for the origin of the universe. Lemaître's work bridged the gap between science and religion, demonstrating that faith and reason are not mutually exclusive but can coexist harmoniously.

Catholic scholars have also made notable contributions to literature and the arts. The works of Dante Alighieri, a 14th-century Italian poet and Catholic intellectual, are considered masterpieces of world literature. His epic poem, the Divine Comedy, explores themes of sin, redemption, and the journey towards God, and has had a profound influence on Western literature and culture.

Catholic scholars have made significant contributions to the development of ethical and moral frameworks. The writings of Catholic social thinkers such as St. Thomas More, St. John Paul II, and Dorothy Day have provided insights into issues of social justice, human rights, and the dignity of the human person. Their work has influenced political movements and has inspired individuals to work towards creating a more just and compassionate society.

Furthermore, Catholic scholars and intellectuals have played a crucial role in the preservation and dissemination of knowledge throughout history. Monastic orders, such as the Benedictines and the Jesuits, have been centers of learning and scholarship, preserving ancient texts and producing new works of knowledge. Catholic universities and educational institutions have also played a vital role in fostering intellectual inquiry and promoting academic excellence.

The contributions of Catholic scholars and intellectuals throughout history have been diverse and far-reaching. Their work has enriched the fields of theology, philosophy, science, literature, and the arts, and has had a profound impact on our understanding of the world and our place in it. Their intellectual pursuits have been guided by a deep faith and a commitment to truth, reason, and the pursuit of knowledge. The legacy of Catholic scholars continues to inspire and shape the intellectual and cultural landscape of today.

Contemporary Challenges and Developments in Catholic Education

Contemporary Catholic education faces a range of challenges and developments that shape its landscape and influence its mission. These challenges arise from societal changes, technological advancements, and evolving educational paradigms. At the same time, there are also exciting developments that present opportunities for growth and innovation in Catholic education.

One of the significant challenges facing Catholic education today is the changing cultural and religious landscape. Society has become more diverse, with an increasing number of students coming from different religious backgrounds or no religious affiliation at all. This diversity presents a challenge for Catholic schools to maintain their distinct identity and effectively transmit Catholic teachings and values to students who may not share the same faith background. It requires a delicate balance of inclusivity, respect for diversity, and fidelity to Catholic teachings.

Another challenge is the increasing secularization of society, which can lead to a decline in religious practice and a diminishing understanding of the importance of faith in education. Catholic schools must find ways to engage students and families in the richness of the Catholic faith, making it relevant and meaningful in their lives. This may involve creative approaches to religious instruction, fostering a vibrant faith community within the school, and providing opportunities for students to live out their faith through service and social justice initiatives.

Technological advancements also present both challenges and opportunities for Catholic education. On one hand, technology can enhance teaching and learning, providing access to a wealth of information and resources. However, it also poses challenges in terms of managing screen time, ensuring digital safety, and maintaining a balance between virtual and face-to-face interactions.

Catholic schools must navigate these challenges while integrating technology in a way that aligns with their mission and values.

In recent years, there has been a growing emphasis on personalized and student-centered learning approaches. This shift in educational paradigms presents an opportunity for Catholic schools to tailor instruction to meet the unique needs and interests of each student. By embracing innovative teaching methods and incorporating individualized learning plans, Catholic schools can foster a more engaging and effective learning environment.

Furthermore, there is a renewed focus on the integration of faith and reason in Catholic education. This involves promoting a dialogue between faith and the various academic disciplines, encouraging critical thinking, and fostering a holistic understanding of the world. Catholic schools are increasingly recognizing the importance of nurturing both the intellectual and spiritual development of students, equipping them with the tools to navigate complex ethical and moral issues.

In response to these challenges and developments, Catholic education is undergoing exciting transformations. Many Catholic schools are embracing a more holistic approach to education, recognizing the importance of educating the whole person—mind, body, and spirit. They are incorporating mindfulness practices, promoting physical well-being, and providing opportunities for spiritual growth and reflection.

Additionally, there is a growing emphasis on community engagement and social justice in Catholic education. Schools are encouraging students to actively participate in service projects, engage with local communities, and advocate for social change. This focus on social responsibility aligns with the Catholic social teaching principles of solidarity, subsidiarity, and the preferential option for the poor.

Moreover, Catholic education is increasingly embracing interfaith dialogue and collaboration. Recognizing the importance of fostering understanding and respect among different religious traditions, Catholic schools are creating opportunities for students to engage in meaningful conversations and learn from diverse perspectives. This promotes a culture of inclusivity and prepares students to be global citizens in an interconnected world.

CHAPTER 14

Catholicism in a Global Context

C atholicism, as one of the largest and most widespread religious traditions in the world, has experienced a remarkable spread and diversity across different continents, countries, and cultures. From its origins in the Mediterranean region, Catholicism has expanded to become a truly global faith, with followers and communities in every corner of the world.

We know that the spread of Catholicism can be traced back to the early days of Christianity when the apostles and early missionaries traveled to various regions to spread the teachings of Jesus Christ. The Roman Empire played a significant role in the early growth of Catholicism, as it provided a network of roads and infrastructure that facilitated the movement of missionaries and the establishment of Christian communities.

One of the key factors in the spread of Catholicism was the conversion of Emperor Constantine to Christianity in the 4th century. This led to the official recognition and support of Christianity within the Roman Empire, which allowed the faith to flourish and expand. Missionaries, such as St. Patrick in Ireland and St. Augustine of Canterbury in England, played a crucial role in bringing Catholicism to new territories.

During the Age of Exploration in the 15th and 16th centuries, Catholicism spread to the Americas, Africa, and Asia through the efforts of European explorers and missionaries. Spanish and Portuguese explorers, in particular, played a significant role in bringing Catholicism to the Americas, establishing missions, and converting indigenous populations. The arrival of Catholicism in the Americas had a profound impact on the cultural, religious, and social landscape of these regions.

In Africa, Catholicism spread through the efforts of missionaries from various religious orders, such as the Jesuits, Franciscans, and Dominicans. These missionaries established schools, hospitals, and churches, and worked to integrate Catholic teachings with local customs and traditions. Today, Africa is home to a vibrant and growing Catholic community, with a significant number of Catholics residing in countries such as Nigeria, the Democratic Republic of Congo, and Uganda.

In Asia, Catholicism has a long and rich history, dating back to the arrival of St. Thomas the Apostle in India in the 1st century. Over the centuries, Catholicism spread to countries such as China, Japan, the Philippines, and Vietnam. The Catholic Church in Asia is characterized by its diversity, with different rites and traditions coexisting within the broader Catholic faith. The growth of Catholicism in Asia has been influenced by a variety of factors, including colonialism, missionary efforts, and the presence of indigenous Christian communities.

Today, Catholicism continues to thrive and grow in different parts of the world, with an estimated 1.3 billion Catholics worldwide. The Catholic Church is organized into various geographical regions, known as dioceses, each led by a bishop. The Pope, as the Bishop of Rome and the head of the Catholic Church, serves as a unifying figure for Catholics around the world.

The diversity of Catholicism is evident in the different rites and traditions that exist within the faith. The Latin Rite, which is the most widespread, is followed by the majority of Catholics. However, there are also Eastern Catholic Churches, which have their own distinct liturgical traditions and practices. These include the Byzantine, Maronite, Coptic, and Syro-Malabar Churches, among others.

Catholicism also embraces cultural diversity, as it has adapted and incorporated local customs and traditions in different regions. This can be seen in the vibrant celebrations of religious festivals, the incorporation of indigenous languages and music in liturgical practices, and the presence of local saints and devotions.

The spread and diversity of Catholicism worldwide is a testament to its enduring appeal and adaptability. From its origins in the Mediterranean region, Catholicism has spread to every continent, with followers and communities in diverse cultural, social, and political contexts. The growth of Catholicism has been influenced by historical events, missionary efforts, and the integration of local customs and traditions. Today, Catholicism continues to be a vibrant and dynamic faith, embracing its global diversity while remaining united in its core beliefs and teachings.

Challenges and Opportunities for Catholicism in Different Cultural and Political Contexts

Catholicism faces a range of challenges and opportunities as it interacts with different cultural and political contexts around the world. The way Catholicism is practiced and perceived can vary greatly depending on the cultural, social, and political environment in which it exists. These contexts present both challenges that need to be navigated and opportunities for growth and engagement.

One challenge is the clash between Catholic teachings and cultural practices or beliefs. In some cultures, certain Catholic teachings may be at odds with deeply ingrained cultural norms or traditions. This can create tension and resistance to the acceptance of Catholic teachings and practices. For example, issues related to gender roles, sexuality, and reproductive rights can be particularly contentious in some cultural contexts.

Another challenge is the presence of other religious traditions and the competition for followers and influence. In multicultural societies, Catholicism often coexists with other religious traditions, and Catholics may face challenges in maintaining and transmitting their faith in the face of alternative belief systems. This can lead to questions of religious identity and the need to engage in interfaith dialogue and understanding.

Additionally, political contexts can present challenges for Catholicism. In some countries, there may be restrictions on religious freedom or government policies that conflict with Catholic teachings. This can limit the ability of the Church to operate freely and can create tensions between the Church and the state. Political ideologies that promote secularism or prioritize individual rights over religious values can also pose challenges for Catholicism.

Opportunities for Catholicism in different cultural and political contexts also exist. One opportunity is the ability to engage in dialogue and bridge cultural and religious divides. Catholicism has a rich tradition of engaging with different cultures and seeking common ground. This can be an opportunity to promote understanding, respect, and cooperation between different religious and cultural communities.

Another opportunity is the potential for social and political engagement. Catholic social teaching emphasizes the importance of social justice, human rights, and the dignity of every person. In different cultural and political contexts, Catholics can play a role in advocating for social change, promoting peace, and addressing issues such as poverty, inequality, and environmental sustainability. The Church's moral authority and global network can be leveraged to make a positive impact in society.

Furthermore, Catholicism can find opportunities for growth and renewal by adapting to cultural contexts while remaining faithful to its core teachings. The Church has a long history of inculturation, which involves integrating local customs, traditions, and languages into the practice of the faith. This can help make Catholicism more accessible and relevant to people in different cultural contexts. It also allows for the development of diverse expressions of Catholicism that reflect the richness of local cultures and traditions.

Technological advancements also present opportunities for Catholicism to reach and engage with people in different cultural and political contexts. The use of digital media, social networks, and online platforms can facilitate communication, education, and evangelization. It can help overcome geographical barriers and connect Catholics across different regions and cultures.

Catholicism faces both challenges and opportunities as it interacts with different cultural and political contexts. Challenges can arise from clashes between Catholic teachings and cultural practices, the presence of other religious traditions, and political restrictions on religious freedom. However, there are also opportunities for dialogue, social and political engagement, and growth through inculturation and the use of technology. By navigating these challenges and embracing these opportunities, Catholicism can continue to be a vibrant and relevant faith in diverse cultural and political contexts around the world.

Intersections Between Catholicism and Global Issues

The intersections between Catholicism and global issues such as migration, environmentalism, and globalization are complex and multifaceted. Catholicism has a significant influence on how its followers engage with these pressing global challenges.

Migration is a topic that has gained increasing attention in recent years. The Catholic Church has a long-standing commitment to welcoming and supporting migrants and refugees. This commitment is rooted in the belief that every human being is made in the image and likeness of God and deserves dignity and respect. Pope Francis, in particular, has been vocal about the need to address the root causes of migration and to create a more just and compassionate response to those who are forced to leave their homes due to conflict, poverty, or persecution.

Environmentalism is another global issue that has become a central concern for the Catholic Church. Pope Francis's encyclical letter, Laudato Si', released in 2015, called for urgent action to address the ecological crisis and its impact on the most vulnerable populations. The document emphasizes the interconnectedness of all creation and the moral responsibility to care for the Earth as a gift from God. The Catholic Church has been actively promoting sustainable practices, advocating for environmental justice, and encouraging individuals and communities to adopt more eco-friendly lifestyles.

Globalization, with its economic, social, and cultural implications, also intersects with Catholicism. The Church recognizes the potential benefits of globalization, such as increased interconnectedness and opportunities for collaboration. However, it also acknowledges the negative consequences, such as economic inequality, exploitation, and the erosion of local cultures and traditions. The Catholic social teaching principles of solidarity, subsidiarity, and the common good provide a framework for engaging with globalization in a way that promotes justice, human dignity, and the well-being of all people.

In addressing these global issues, the Catholic Church often collaborates with other religious and secular organizations, governments, and civil society groups. It seeks to build bridges and foster dialogue to find common ground and work towards solutions that promote human flourishing and the common good. The Church's engagement with these issues is not limited to theoretical discussions but also involves practical action, such as providing humanitarian aid, advocating for policy changes, and supporting grassroots initiatives.

It is important to note that while the Catholic Church provides guidance and moral teachings on these global issues, individual Catholics may have different perspectives and interpretations. The

Church encourages dialogue and discernment, recognizing that there can be a diversity of approaches and solutions within the framework of Catholic social teaching.

The intersections between Catholicism and global issues such as migration, environmentalism, and globalization are significant and complex. The Catholic Church, through its teachings and actions, seeks to address these challenges in a way that promotes justice, compassion, and the well-being of all people. By engaging with these issues, Catholics are called to live out their faith and contribute to building a more just and sustainable world.

CHAPTER 15

The Future of Catholicism

T he future of Catholicism presents both prospects and challenges as the Church navigates a rapidly changing world. While the Church faces various challenges, it also possesses strengths and opportunities that can shape its future.

Prospects:

- **Global Presence:** Catholicism is a global religion with a presence in diverse regions and cultures. This global reach provides opportunities for the Church to engage with different perspectives, learn from diverse experiences, and foster a sense of unity among believers worldwide.

- **Social Justice Advocacy:** The Catholic Church has a strong tradition of social justice advocacy. Its commitment to promoting human dignity, addressing poverty, and advocating for the marginalized positions it well to continue making a positive impact in society.

- **Youth Engagement:** Engaging younger generations is crucial for the future of Catholicism. The Church has the opportunity to connect with young people, address their spiritual needs, and provide spaces for their active participation and leadership within the Church.

- **Interfaith Dialogue:** The Catholic Church has made significant strides in interfaith dialogue, fostering understanding and collaboration with other religious traditions. This engagement can contribute to peacebuilding, mutual respect, and the promotion of shared values in an increasingly interconnected world.

Challenges:

- **Declining Membership:** Like many religious institutions, the Catholic Church faces declining membership in some regions. Factors such as secularization, changing societal attitudes, and the influence of individualism contribute to this challenge. The Church must find ways to engage with younger generations and address their spiritual needs to reverse this trend.

- **Cultural and Societal Changes:** The Church operates within a rapidly changing cultural and societal context. It faces challenges in adapting to new technologies, addressing issues such as gender equality and LGBTQ+ rights, and engaging with diverse cultural and religious traditions while remaining faithful to its core teachings.

- **Internal Unity and Reform:** The Catholic Church is a diverse institution with differing perspectives on various issues. Internal conflicts and divisions can pose challenges to unity and effective decision-making. The Church must navigate these challenges through dialogue, discernment, and a commitment to finding common ground.

- **Clergy Shortages:** The shortage of priests in many regions poses challenges for the availability of pastoral care and sacraments. The Church must address this issue by promoting vocations, exploring new models of ministry, and empowering laypeople to take on greater roles within the Church.

Addressing these challenges and capitalizing on prospects requires a commitment to ongoing dialogue, discernment, and adaptation. The Church must continue to engage with the world, listen to diverse voices, and respond to the needs of the faithful. It must continue to foster a culture of transparency, accountability, and compassion, while remaining faithful to its core teachings and values.

In navigating the future, the Catholic Church can draw upon its rich theological tradition, the guidance of the Magisterium, and the commitment of its members. It can leverage its global presence, social justice advocacy, and engagement with young people and other religious traditions to shape a future that reflects its mission of spreading the Gospel, promoting justice, and serving the needs of all people.

Emerging Trends in Catholic Theology, Spirituality, and Practice

Emerging trends in Catholic theology, spirituality, and practice reflect the ongoing evolution and adaptation of the Catholic Church in response to the changing needs and contexts of the modern world. These trends encompass a range of developments that shape the way Catholics understand and live out their faith.

Let's explore some of the emerging trends in Catholic theology, spirituality, and practice, to understand them better:

- **Inculturation and Contextual Theology:** There is a growing emphasis on inculturation and contextual theology within Catholicism. This trend recognizes the importance of integrating local cultures, traditions, and experiences into the expression of faith. It seeks to bridge the gap between the universal teachings of the Church and the particularities of diverse cultural contexts, allowing for a more authentic and relevant experience of Catholicism.

- **Ecological Theology and Care for Creation:** The recognition of the ecological crisis has led to an emerging trend of ecological theology and care for creation within Catholicism. This trend emphasizes the interconnectedness of all creation and the responsibility of humans to be stewards of the Earth. It calls for a holistic approach to environmental issues, integrating ecological concerns into theological reflection, liturgical practices, and ethical decision-making.

• **Interreligious Dialogue and Interfaith Engagement:** The Catholic Church is increasingly engaged in interreligious dialogue and interfaith engagement. This trend recognizes the importance of building bridges of understanding, promoting mutual respect, and working collaboratively with people of different religious traditions. It seeks to foster dialogue, address shared concerns, and promote peace and social justice in a diverse and pluralistic world.

• **Emphasis on Social Justice and Integral Human Development:** There is a renewed emphasis on social justice and integral human development within Catholic theology and practice. This trend recognizes the Church's responsibility to address systemic injustices, promote human dignity, and work towards the common good. It calls for a holistic approach to social issues, integrating spiritual, social, and political dimensions in the pursuit of justice and the well-being of all individuals and communities.

• **Lay Empowerment and Co-Responsibility:** There is a growing recognition of the importance of lay empowerment and co-responsibility within the Catholic Church. This trend seeks to involve laypeople more actively in the life of the Church, encouraging their participation in decision-making, leadership roles, and ministries. It recognizes the unique gifts and perspectives that laypeople bring to the Church and seeks to foster a sense of shared responsibility for the mission of the Church.

• **Embracing Diversity and Inclusivity:** There is an increasing emphasis on embracing diversity and inclusivity within Catholicism. This trend recognizes the dignity and worth of every individual, regardless of their background, race, gender, or sexual orientation. It calls for a more welcoming and inclusive Church that values the contributions and experiences of all its members.

- **Integration of Technology and Digital Media:** The integration of technology and digital media is an emerging trend in Catholic practice and outreach. This trend recognizes the potential of technology to enhance communication, evangelization, and community-building. It involves the use of social media, online platforms, and digital resources to engage with individuals, share the Gospel, and foster spiritual growth.

These emerging trends reflect the ongoing development and adaptation of Catholic theology, spirituality, and practice in response to the needs and challenges of the modern world. They seek to foster a more inclusive, relevant, and engaged expression of Catholicism that addresses the complexities of contemporary life while remaining faithful to the core teachings and values of the Church.

Conclusion

Exploring the sacred traditions of Catholic beliefs and practices provides a deeper understanding of Catholicism as a rich and multifaceted religious tradition. From its foundational beliefs in the Holy Trinity, the divinity of Jesus Christ, and the authority of the Church, to its sacramental life, liturgical worship, and moral teachings, Catholicism encompasses a comprehensive framework for spiritual growth and engagement with the world.

By delving into the history, theology, and rituals of Catholicism, we can appreciate the profound significance of the Eucharist, the power of the sacraments, and the role of Mary and the saints in Catholic devotion. The Catholic Church's commitment to social justice, care for the poor and marginalized, and the pursuit of peace also reflects its core values and teachings.

Understanding Catholicism goes beyond mere knowledge; it invites one to embrace a personal relationship with God, to participate in a vibrant faith community, and to live out the Gospel values in their daily life. It encourages a spirit of inquiry, dialogue, and ongoing formation, as Catholics seek to deepen their understanding of their faith and its relevance to contemporary issues.

Moreover, exploring Catholicism can foster interfaith dialogue and understanding, as it shares common ground with other Christian denominations and engages in dialogue with other religious traditions. By appreciating the diversity within Catholicism, including its various rites, devotions, and cultural expressions, one can recognize the universality and adaptability of the Catholic faith.

Ultimately, understanding Catholicism is a journey of discovery, reflection, and growth. It invites individuals to explore the depths of their own spirituality, to engage with the wisdom of the Church's tradition, and to seek a deeper relationship with God and their fellow human beings. Whether one is a lifelong Catholic, a curious seeker, or an interfaith explorer, the exploration of Catholic belief and practice offers a pathway to spiritual enrichment, intellectual engagement, and a deeper understanding of the sacred mysteries of life and faith.

References

ABOUT | True Holiness. (n.d.). True Holiness. https://www.trueholinessglobal.org/about

Adeline. (2022, June 16). Conversion to Christianity - Church my way. *Church My Way.* https://churchmyway.org/conversion-to-christianity/

Atlanticchurch. (2023, June 27). *The Origin of Church - atlantic church.* Atlantic Church. https://www.atlanticchurch.com/the-origin-of-church/

Bennett to Senate: Protect religious freedom. (2016, December 13). https://www.convivium.ca/articles/bennett-to-senate-protect-religious-freedom/

Blogsupport. (2023, June 30). In vitro fertilization and its ethical dilemmas. *Blissful Faith Inc.* https://www.blissfulfaithblog.com/post/in-vitro-fertilization-and-it-s-ethical-dilemmas

catholic sacraments - The Catholic Foodie. (n.d.). The Catholic Foodie. https://www.catholicfoodie.com/tag/catholic-sacraments/

catholic teaching orders. (n.d.). http://crowebrothers.com/oanda-broker-itxgef/catholic-teaching-orders-cbb8ab

Churchreaders. (2023, April 2). Catholic Confession Guide: In the Acrament of Reconciliation. *Church Readers.* https://churchreaders.com/catholic-confession-guide-understanding-and-participating-in-the-sacrament-of-reconciliation/

Confirmation. (n.d.). Queen of Peace Catholic Church. https://queenofpeace.cc/confirmation

Dooley. (2021, February 25). *Anointing of the sick - St Anthonys.* St Anthonys. https://www.stanthonykenosha.org/sacraments/anointing-of-the-sick/

Flyverbom, M., & Reinecke, J. (2017). The Spectacle and organization studies. *Organization Studies*, *38*(11), 1625–1643. https://doi.org/10.1177/0170840616685366

Gibson, I., & Gibson, I. (2024, January 11). *Discover the answers to the top 10 questions about Christianity!* God Liberation Cathedral. https://gibsnet.com/discover-the-answers-to-the-top-10-questions-about-christianity/

Hayes, E. J. (2023a, September 19). Catholic Social Teaching: Parishes and Catholic Beliefs. *Catholics Come Home Boston*. https://catholicscomehomeboston.org/catholic-social-teaching/

Hayes, E. J. (2023b, September 19). Penance in Parishes: Catholic sacraments. *Catholics Come Home Boston*. https://catholicscomehomeboston.org/penance/

Hayes, E. J. (2023c, September 19). The Anointing of the Sick: a Catholic sacrament in parishes. *Catholics Come Home Boston*. https://catholicscomehomeboston.org/anointing-of-the-sick/

Holy Orders | Saint Joseph. (n.d.). Saint Joseph. https://www.stjosephogden.org/holy-orders

Holy Orders · St. Dominic Catholic Church. (n.d.). https://www.saintdominicpc.com/sacraments/holy-orders

How did christianity spread throughout the roman empire. (2023, September 19). Sorumatik. https://sorumatik.co/t/how-did-christianity-spread-throughout-the-roman-empire/22120

Jordan, J. M. (2023, June 14). *Catholics vs. Protestants vs. Lutheran: What is the main difference?* Christian Faith Guide. https://christianfaithguide.com/catholics-vs-protestants-vs-lutheran/

Kristen, & Kristen. (2023a, June 24). 8 Questions about Catholicism: Answered - Catholic Mom Journey. *Catholic Mom Blog - The Catholic Mom Journey*. https://catholicmomjourney.com/my-journey/questions-about-catholicism/

Kristen, & Kristen. (2023b, July 10). 6 Common Questions about a Catholic Pope - Catholic Mom blog. *Catholic Mom Blog - The Catholic Mom Journey*. https://catholicmomjourney.com/my-journey/catholic-pope-questions/

PCV Editor. (n.d.). *The progressive Catholic Voice*. https://theprogressivecatholicvoice.blogspot.com/2010/07/

Rains, R., & Rains, R. (2023, August 13). *Expressions of Faith Through Music: Modern Examples and Inspirations | Fabrizio bosso*. Fabrizio Bosso. https://www.fabriziobosso.com/expressions-of-faith-through-music-modern-examples-and-inspirations.htm

Saxone. (2023, June 27). What are followers of Christianity called? - Christian Gist. *Christian Gist*. https://christiangist.com/what-are-followers-of-christianity-called/

Seaford Shores. (2023, June 18). *How to Pray to the Rosary - Seaford Shores*. https://seaforddecor.com/portfolio/how-to-pray-to-the-rosary/

Stephen. (2023a, August 13). Breaking Barriers: The Fight for Women's Suffrage in the 19th Century - 19th Century. *Semilla de Botjael*. https://19thcentury.us/womens-suffrage-in-19th-century/

Stephen, O. (2023b, September 17). How to live a Catholic life in the modern world - AMC4L. *AMC4L*. https://amcatholic4life.com/how-to-live-a-catholic-life-in-the-modern-world/

Teaching Catholic Kids. (n.d.). *Holy Saturday Archives - Teaching Catholic kids*. https://www.teachingcatholickids.com/tag/holy-saturday/

The Ethiopian Church. (n.d.). Nine Saints Ethiopian Orthodox Monastery. https://ninesaintsethiopianorthodoxmonastery.org/

The growth of Christianity in Ancient Rome. (n.d.). http://www.history4kids.co/2017/01/the-growth-of-christianity-in-ancient-Rome.html

The Universal Church of the Restoration. (n.d.). *John the Baptist Archives - Universal Restoration Ministries*. Universal Restoration Ministries. https://universalrestoration.org/tag/john-the-baptist/

What is a Permanent Deacon & His Role. (2023, August 16). Holyfamily. https://www.holyfamilylatrobe.org/post/what-is-a-permanent-deacon-his-role

Made in the USA
Columbia, SC
21 November 2024

4406c72f-e9c8-4424-8b3f-2c78d63e2fa0R01